Formal Verification of Concurrent Embedded Software

M.Sc. Johannes Frederik Jesper Traub

Dissertation
zur Erlangung des akademischen Grades
Doktor der Ingenieurwissenschaften
(Dr.-Ing.)
der Technischen Fakultät
der Christian-Albrechts-Universität zu Kiel
eingereicht im Jahr 2015

Kiel Computer Science Series (KCSS) 2016/1 v1.0 dated 2016-02-04

ISSN 2193-6781 (print version)
ISSN 2194-6639 (electronic version)

Electronic version, updates, errata available via https://www.informatik.uni-kiel.de/kcss

Published by the Department of Computer Science, Kiel University

Dependable Systems Group

Please cite as:

▷ Johannes Frederik Jesper Traub. *Formal Verification of Concurrent Embedded Software*. Number 2016/1 in Kiel Computer Science Series. Department of Computer Science, 2016. Dissertation, Faculty of Engineering, Kiel University.

```
@book{JFJTraub,
  author    = {Johannes Frederik Jesper Traub},
  title     = {Formal Verification of Concurrent Embedded Software},
  publisher = {Department of Computer Science, CAU Kiel},
  year      = {2016},
  number    = {2016/1},
  isbn      = {978-3-7392-4124-1},
  series    = {Kiel Computer Science Series},
  note      = {Dissertation, Faculty of Engineering, Kiel University.}
}
```

Herstellung und Verlag: BoD — Books on Demand, Norderstedt

ISBN 978-3-7392-4124-1

About this Series

The Kiel Computer Science Series (KCSS) covers dissertations, habilitation theses, lecture notes, textbooks, surveys, collections, handbooks, etc. written at the Department of Computer Science at Kiel University. It was initiated in 2011 to support authors in the dissemination of their work in electronic and printed form, without restricting their rights to their work. The series provides a unified appearance and aims at high-quality typography. The KCSS is an open access series; all series titles are electronically available free of charge at the department's website. In addition, authors are encouraged to make printed copies available at a reasonable price, typically with a print-on-demand service.

Please visit http://www.informatik.uni-kiel.de/kcss for more information, for instructions how to publish in the KCSS, and for access to all existing publications.

1. Gutachter: Prof. Dr. Dirk Nowotka
                     Christian-Albrechts-Universität zu Kiel

2. Gutachter: Prof. Dr. Martin Leuker
                     Universität zu Lübeck

Datum der mündlichen Prüfung: 21.12.2015

Zusammenfassung

Software, die im automobilen Umfeld eingesetzt wird, hat in der Regel mit sicherheitskritischen Systemen zu tun. Aus diesem Grund ist die funktionale Korrektheit der Software von großer Bedeutung. Ein Mittel zum Nachweis derselben ist die Statische Software Analyse, welche Laufzeitfehler in Software identifizieren kann und ein Standard im Automobilbereich geworden ist. Der kritischste Laufzeitfehler ist einer, der nur sporadisch auftritt und daher nur sehr schwer auffindbar und reproduzierbar ist. Eine Ursache für einen solchen Fehler ist zum Beispiel eine Race Condition. Die Einführung von Multicore Hardware erlaubt eine tatsächliche parallele Ausführung der Software, was zur Folge hat, dass die Wahrscheinlichkeit für das Vorkommen einer kritischen Race Condition zunimmt.

In der vorliegenden Thesis wird MEMICS, ein Ansatz zur Verifikation von Software, vorgestellt. Um genaue Ergebnisse zu erzielen, arbeitet MEMICS basierend auf Bounded Model Checking, einer Technik aus dem Bereich der formalen Verifikation. Das interne Modell kann ein Steuergerät aus der Automobil-Branche inklusive der Hardware-Konfiguration und des dazugehörigen Betriebssystems, zum Beispiel AUTOSAR oder OSEK, abbilden. Die Verifikations-Einheit in MEMICS ist ein neu entwickelter Interval Constraint Solver mit einem integrierten Speichermodell. MEMICS kann sowohl herkömmliche Laufzeitfehler, wie eine Division durch Null, als auch nebenläufige Laufzeitfehler, zum Beispiel eine kritische Race Condition, identifizieren.

Abstract

Automotive software is mainly concerned with safety critical systems and the functional correctness of the software is very important. Thus static software analysis, being able to detect runtime errors in software, has become a standard in the automotive domain. The most critical runtime error is one which only occurs sporadically and is therefore very difficult to detect and reproduce. A reason for such an error is e. g., a race condition. The introduction of multicore hardware enables an execution of the software in real parallel. Hence, the risk of critical race conditions increases.

This thesis introduces the MEMICS software verification approach. In order to produce precise results, MEMICS works based on the formal verification technique, bounded model checking. The internal model is able to represent an entire automotive control unit, including the hardware configuration as well as real-time operating systems like AUTOSAR and OSEK. The proof engine used to check the model is a newly developed interval constraint solver with an embedded memory model. MEMICS is able to detect common runtime errors, like e. g., a division by zero, as well as concurrent ones, like e. g., a critical race condition.

Acknowledgements

First of all I want to thank my supervisor Prof. Dr. Dirk Nowotka for his mentoring and his survey as well as for his intensive and competent support and collaboration. His expert advice was instrumental in the success of this work. In addition I am grateful for the freedom he gave me during my research. Thank you very much!

I also thank the Daimler AG for allowing me to fully commit myself to this work. I want to thank all my colleges at the Daimler AG, especially Dr. Steffen Görzig, as well as all colleges at the Dependable Systems Group for their interest in my work, numerous motivating discussions on and off topic and several activities in their free time.

Last but not least I want to thank my entire family and friends for their support, particularly my wife, who encouraged me during the period of this work, including all ups and downs.

Johannes F. J. Traub
Stuttgart, February 2016

Contents

Contents

List of Figures

List of Figures

List of Tables

Listings

Chapter 1

Introduction

Most of the new features – invented in the past few decades – in the automotive domain are based on embedded systems, the so-called electronic control units (ECUs). These ECUs are mainly driven by software and are e. g., used in the following areas:

1. Powertrain Electronics: Most common usage is the engine- and transmission-control.

2. Chassis Electronics: Monitoring of several safety critical systems, like the anti-lock braking system (ABS) or the electronic stability program (ESP).

3. Driver Assistance: Management of several assist systems, like a lane assist, an adaptive cruise control (ACC), or a park assist.

4. Active Safety: Most common feature is the airbag-control.

5. Infotainment Systems: Management of the navigation system, in-car audio/video and so on.

Many of these systems are safety critical, since a malfunction has the potential to risk human life. Hence, there exists a standard demanding for the functional correctness of the software used in these ECUs. In order to guarantee a correct functional behavior of the software one of the techniques postulated by this standard is the application of static software analysis. In static software analysis the software is analyzed for all different kind of runtime errors without executing the software itself. Since the amount of software used in the automotive domain is growing very fast, the analysis tools must be able to handle up to several million lines of source code. Therefore, most of them work with some kinds of abstraction mechanisms. Hence, the consequence is a lack of precision in their output. Thus, a manual review of the error candidates is necessary. Since most of the ECUs control time critical features, their basis is a real-time operating system implementing several tasks with different priorities. These tasks can interrupt each other depending on their priority, which results in a concurrent execution. This concurrent execution can cause one of the most critical types of runtime errors, the so-called race conditions. Such a race condition is e. g., the concurrent access to the same hardware resource from two different tasks. These race conditions usually only occur sporadically and are therefore very difficult to detect and reproduce. Since an analysis tool has to report any possible race condition over the entire software, the result is an even bigger number of error candidates.

It is not only the software, which is evolving very quickly in the automotive domain, but also is the hardware. The latest innovation in the past few years, is the introduction of multicore hardware to the automotive domain. This new hardware allows the software to be truly executed in parallel. Thus, the probability for critical race conditions increases strongly. Simultaneously, a real parallel execution of software results in more possible interleavings of tasks. Hence, with the strongly increasing amount of error candidates, a manual review is in most cases not feasible any more.

This thesis introduces Memory Interval Constraint Solving (MEMICS), a new software verification approach. MEMICS is able to detect common runtime errors in C/C++ source code, as well as critical concurrent ones. The main goal of MEMICS is to offer precise results. Therefore, it is working based on formal verification, using a technique called bounded model checking. To offer even more precision its internal model is based on an assembly language, instead of directly on the high-level languages C/C++. In addition this model offers structures to configure the entire ECU, including the operating system with tasks, interrupts, and so on, as well as parts of the actual hardware. In order to reduce the search space, MEMICS is equipped with an efficient unrolling mechanism. The heart of the approach itself is a newly developed interval constraint solver with an embedded memory model.

The foundations required in this thesis are located in Chapter 2, including the related work section. In Chapter 3 the new software verification approach

(MEMICS) is introduced in detail. The results of test cases, with an additional comparison to related state of the art tools, and the according discussion is located in Chapter 4. An industrial tool-chain is introduced in Chapter 5, in which MEMICS is used to investigate error candidates produced from industrial static software analysis tools. The conclusion and future work is located in Chapter 6.

Chapter 2

Foundations

2.1 Automotive Software

Automotive software is often implemented in the programming languages C
[1] or C++ [2]. In this work the term software is restricted to the executable
code and nothing else, like e. g., documentation. The focus of this work is – as
aforementioned – on the functional correctness of the implemented software,
especially on safety critical systems. Since most of these systems have to meet
specific timing constraints, they are mainly implemented in real-time systems.

Real-Time Systems

A real-time system [3, 4] has to meet strict timing requirements. The main difference between real-time software and other programs is in their definition of
functional correctness. For a common program functional correctness is defined
by the valid result of the implemented function(s). In the case of real-time software, functional correctness is defined by the correct result and the amount of
time required to compute it.

Such real-time systems are often built on a task basis, where each task is
scheduled in a defined time slot and has to provide some functionality in defined
deadlines. A common example of such a real-time system is OSEK, which is used
in the automotive domain.

2.1.1 OSEK

In the year 1993 the standard "Open Systems and their Interfaces for the Electronics in Motor Vehicles" (OSEK) [5, 6] was introduced by a consortium composed

of original equipment manufactures (OEMs) from the automotive domain and Tier 1 suppliers. Since this time, the OSEK-OS has been used as a basis in almost any electronic control unit (ECU) in the automotive domain. The standard provides a lot of features to describe and build task based real-time systems. Another main standard introduced by the OSEK consortium is the "OSEK Implementation Language" (OIL) [7]. This implementation language represents the standard system configuration. It includes the specification of tasks, interrupts, events, resources and so on. Each of the tasks in OSEK has a certain priority. The scheduler of OSEK uses this priority for the execution of tasks. The task – waiting for execution – with the highest priority is selected by the scheduler. In order to avoid problems like deadlocks or priority inversion, OSEK uses the priority ceiling protocol [8, 9], for details see [6]. Since this standard is quite old, the configuration is for single CPUs, only.

2.1.2 AUTOSAR

Ten years after the introduction of OSEK, in the year 2003, the standard "Automotive Open System Architecture" (AUTOSAR) [10] was founded by a consortium – consisting of almost the same contributors like in the OSEK case. The main goal of AUTOSAR was to introduce a middleware in between the OS with its basic software (BSW) and the actual application software (ASW). In addition this introduction had two major purposes to provide a standard OS and BSW, as well as to support the migratability, maintainability and replaceability of the ASW. The OS in AUTOSAR is built on the basis of OSEK. The introduced middleware is represented by the Run-Time Environment (RTE), which defines the application programming interface (API) for the ASW towards the OS and its BSW. In addition, the AUTOSAR standard introduces the software components (SWC), in which the ASW has to be partitioned. Such a SWC has to feature defined input- and output-interfaces. According to the standard it is only allowed to access global resources (e. g., signals, variables, etc.) via these interfaces using the RTE. Since the version 4.0 the AUTOSAR standard raises the challenge to tackle the handling of multicore systems.

2.2 Software Quality

In the automotive domain the ISO 26262 [11] is a standard regarding functional safety. The criticality regarding functional safety differs by the impact of a possible failure. Hence, there exists a classification to ensure the reduction towards a reasonable risk of failure in relation to its impact, which is called the Automotive Safety Integrity Level (ASIL) [11]. The determination of the required ASIL – ASIL A, ASIL B, ASIL C or ASIL D – for a product is achieved by risk analysis. ASIL D demands the highest safety requirements and ASIL A the lowest. An example for each ASIL is given in Table 2.1.

Table 2.1. Examples for each ASIL

ASIL	Component	Risk
A	Window Regulator	Entrapment of Limbs
B	Engine Control Unit	Unintentional Acceleration
C	Electronic Stability Control	Faulty Triggering of Brake System
D	Steering Wheel	Faulty Lock while Driving

The aim of the ISO 26262 is to provide a reference process for the product development, including mandatory tasks and methods to ensure functional safety for the acquired ASIL. This reference process is split up into several different phases starting with the management of functional safety, a concept phase, the product development phase, until the actual production and operation. Each phase is again divided into different levels, like e. g., the product development phase is split into the system-level, the hardware- and the software-level. The reference process for the software-level is built based on the state of the art V-model [12, 13] as illustrated in Figure 2.1.

This V-model is defined over several stages starting after the system design and finally leading towards the integration of a software item into the entire system and the corresponding tests. In general there exist two phases in the V-model, the design phase illustrated on the left axis of the V and the test phase shown on the right axis. The software design phase is split up into the stages:

2. Foundations

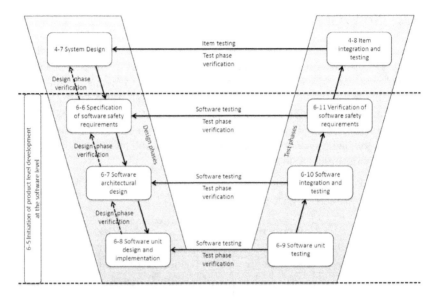

Figure 2.1. The Reference Process of the ISO 26262-6: V-Model of the Software Development Process. [1]

1. Specification of software safety requirements,

2. Software architecture design, and

3. Software unit design and implementation.

The "initiation of the product level development at the software level" starts before point 1 and guides the entire design phase. After each stage of the design phase a verification process checks if the requirements of the prior stage are still covered. In case of unresolvable inconsistencies, the previous stage must be refined properly. Once the design phase is finished and the software has been implemented the testing phase starts. The software testing phase is divided into the stages:

---

[1]The numbers refer to the corresponding section in the ISO 26262-6.

1. Software unit testing,

2. Software integration and testing, and

3. Verification of software safety requirements.

As in the design phase, each step of the testing phase is again concluded by a verification process. The result of this verification however, does not have an impact on the direct prior stage, but on the corresponding counterpart in the design phase. The later a problem occurs during the testing phases, the longer the entire development process can be delayed, which might have a direct impact on the product cost.

The ISO 26262 provides at least one list of criteria for each stage of the Software V, containing several methods regarding the application and verification of the stage. In addition such a list features the recommendations for each method according to the required ASIL. For the stage "Software unit design and implementation" there exist the three lists of criteria: 7, 8, and 9. Regarding software quality table 9 is the most interesting one. It lists the methods for the corresponding verification process and is shown in Table 2.2.

Table 2.2. ISO 26262-6: Table 9 – Methods for the Verification of Software Unit Design and Implementation (Notation: ++ = highly recommended, + = recommended, and o = no recommendation for or against)

| | Methods | ASIL | | | |
		A	B	C	D
1a	Walk-through	++	+	o	o
1b	Inspection	+	++	++	++
1c	Semi-formal verification	+	+	++	++
1d	Formal verification	o	o	+	+
1e	Control flow analysis	+	+	++	++
1f	Data flow analysis	+	+	++	++
1g	Static code analysis	+	++	++	++
1h	Semantic code analysis	+	+	+	+

The two methods "Walk-through" (1a) and "Inspection" (1b) represent a manual analysis or review. These methods can be applied at source code level as well as at model level, in case of model-based software development. "Semi-formal verification"(1c) does not require a complete proof of certain properties. This method often contains software testing. In contrast, the method "Formal verification" (1d) requires a complete proof of a certain property. A common example for this method is Model Checking, which is introduced in Section 2.4.3. The methods "Control flow analysis" (1e) and "Data flow analysis" (1f) are described in Section 2.4.2 and are often part of the methods 1d, 1g and 1h. "Static code analysis" (1g) – or static software analysis – is introduced in Section 2.4. The last method "Semantic code analysis" (1h) refers to a mathematical analysis of source code by use of the method Abstract Interpretation, which is described in Section 2.4.1. All methods listed in this table do not require the execution of the source code and are used to identify code defects.

2.3 Code/Software Defects

Code/Software defects – or bugs – are errors in the implementation of software and result in software behavior violating the specification – e. g., a runtime error. There exists a wide range of runtime errors from which software can suffer, including the categories:

1) Arithmetic, 2) Memory, 3) Pointer Arithmetic, and 4) Concurrent.

The common weakness enumeration database (CWE) [14] covers known categories of code defects. For each defect one can find at least one reference – including proper documentation of the defect, a source code example and a description of its impact. Table 2.3 shows those runtime errors, which are relevant for this work.

The class of arithmetic runtime errors covers defects like e. g., an arithmetic overflow or a division by zero. The coverage of the classes memory and pointer arithmetic is straightforward. The last category – concurrent runtime errors – contains those runtime errors, which are the hardest to detect.

Table 2.3. List of relevant Runtime Errors for this Work. Details on each Error can be found in the Common Weakness Enumeration Database (http://cwe.mitre.org)

	Class	Runtime Error	CWE-ID
1)	Arithmetic	Division By Zero (Floating Point)	369
		Division By Zero (Integer)	369
		Signed Overflow	190
		Signed Underflow	191
2)	Memory	Double Free	415
		Invalid Free	590
		Null Dereference	476
		Pointer To Stack	465
		Size-of On Pointers	467
		Use After Free	416
3)	Pointer Arithmetic	Invalid Range	466
		Scaling	468
		Subtraction	469
4)	Concurrent	Dead Lock	833
		Double Lock	667
		Lost Update	567[2]
		Missing Synchronization	820

2.3.1 Concurrent Code Defects

The class of concurrent code defects covers the most difficult runtime errors. Although deadlocks, double locks and missing synchronization are quite simple to detect – e. g., using pattern matching techniques –, race conditions like e. g., a lost update are not. The hardest task in the detection of such a race condition is that in most of the cases the actual error only occurs sporadically and is therefore very difficult to reproduce.

---

[2]Please note, the exact wording on CWE is not "Lost Update", but the scenario described in the error defines exactly a Lost Update

2. Foundations

2.3.1 Example (A Race Condition in Automotive Software).
A common use case of software in the automotive environment, is e. g., an ECU used for object recognition. Therefore, the car is equipped with a 360° camera, which stores the image of one run in a buffer of size n. A common algorithm to identify objects in such a buffer is the Laplace operator [15]. It computes the difference of each pixel with its corresponding left and right pixels. If this difference is not zero, an object has been identified. Figure 2.2 gives an example of such a buffer for a given image.

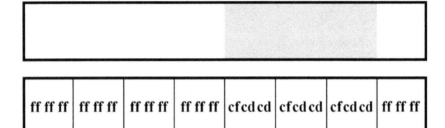

| ff ff ff | ff ff ff | ff ff ff | ff ff ff | cf cd cd | cf cd cd | cf cd cd | ff ff ff |

Figure 2.2. An Example of an 1D Image-Buffer for Edge-Recognition with the Laplace-Operator: On top the actual Image is shown, and below the Buffer with the Hex Values of each Pixel.

The top of the figure shows the image itself and the bottom line represents the hexadecimal value of each pixel. The algorithm of the Laplace operator for the pixel i is defined as:

$$result[i] = buffer[i-1] - 2*buffer[i] + buffer[i+1];$$

Table 2.4 shows the results of the Laplace operator applied to the values from the image buffer of Figure 2.2. The Laplace operator detects both of the edges from the object one pixel in advance.

Table 2.4. The Laplace Operator for the Image-Buffer from Figure 2.2.

Buffer[i]	ffffff	ffffff	ffffff	ffffff	cfcdcd	cfcdcd	cfcdcd	ffffff
Laplace[i]	0	0	0	-303232	303232	0	303232	-303232

An example for an automotive software component implementing this algorithm is shown in Listing 2.1. The component consists of three parts. In the first part, the image buffer is copied into a local buffer. The actual computation of the Laplace operator is implemented in the second part. And in the last part the results are assigned to the output interface of the software component, which can then be used from other components for further purposes – e.g., to track the movement of objects. The CPU of the ECU is an AURIX™ TC277T, which lends itself for parallelization. The tasks for reading the image buffer (readInputs) and assigning the output interface (writeOutputs) are working on the same core, since they do not interact with each other. The actual computation of the Laplace operator is distributed over two separate tasks: worker1 and worker2, where each of these tasks is running on a separate core. To achieve a proper scheduling the events data1Ready, data2Ready, worker1Ready and worker2Ready are used. Once readInputs has read the first half of the buffer, it triggers worker1 and respectively worker2 at the end. The two workers fire an event once they are finished, which triggers the output routine.

Listing 2.1. The Source Code of the Software Component Used for Object Recognition

```
1   #define nSens ExtInput
2
3   int actors[nSens], sensors[nSens], tmp[nSens];
4   int data1Ready, data2Ready;
5   int worker1Ready, worker2Ready;
6
7   extern void clearEvent(int *event);
8   extern void triggerEvent(int *event);
9
10  int readSensor(int index) {
11    int value;
12    return value;
13  }
14
15  int left(int index, int size) {
16    return (index - 1 + size) % size;
17  }
```

```
18
19  int right(int index, int size) {
20    return (index + 1) % size;
21  }
22
23  void readInputs() {
24    clearEvent(&data1Ready);
25    clearEvent(&data2Ready);
26    int i = 0;
27    for(; i < nSens/2 ; i++)
28      sensors[i] = readSensor(i);
29    triggerEvent(&data1Ready);
30    for (; i < nSens; i++)
31      sensors[i] = readSensor(i);
32    triggerEvent(&data2Ready);
33  }
34
35  void writeOutputs() {
36    waitOnEvent(worker1Ready);
37    waitOnEvent(worker2Ready);
38    int i = 0;
39    for(; i < nSens ; i++)
40      actors[i] = tmp[i];
41  }
42
43  void worker1() {
44    clearEvent(&worker1Ready);
45    waitOnEvent(data1Ready);
46    int i=0;
47    int range = nSens / 2;
48    for(; i < range ; i++)
49      tmp[i] = sensors[left(i, nSens)] - 2 * sensors[i] +
50              sensors[right(i, nSens)];
51    triggerEvent(&worker1Ready);
52  }
```

```
53
54  void worker2() {
55    clearEvent(&worker2Ready);
56    waitOnEvent(data2Ready);
57    int i = (nSens / 2);
58    for(; i < nSens ; i++)
59      tmp[i] = sensors[left(i, nSens)] - 2 * sensors[i] +
60              sensors[right(i, nSens)];
61    triggerEvent(&worker2Ready);
62  }
```

On first sight the implementation seems to be well-formed, although it contains a critical race condition. The problem has its origin in the combination of the software being mapped to the hardware and the definition of the Laplace operator itself. Since it computes the difference of each pixel with its corresponding neighbors – the left and right one –, the left neighbor of the first pixel in the buffer is the last pixel in the buffer. But in the current scenario the Laplace operator for the first pixel is computed once the first half of the image buffer is read – and if the corresponding processor core is idle. Hence, there exists a scenario, in which the left pixel still contains the old value. In this case, an edge can be missed.

This example is used as a running example in this work, whenever an example is required for demonstration purposes.

2.4 Code Defect Analysis

In code defect analysis – or program/software analysis – the software is analyzed for the occurrence of any kind of runtime error, like one of those introduced in Table 2.3. There exist two different types of analysis approaches: dynamic and static. In dynamic software analysis the software is checked while executing it on either a real or a virtual system. Contrary to that the software is analyzed

2. Foundations

without being executed in static software analysis. Please note, for the rest of this work the term software analysis refers to static software analysis, only.

Software analysis in general is limited by the following two theorems:

Undecidability of the Halting Problem and Rice's Theorem

The Halting Problem [16] is the decision problem, whether an algorithm terminates or runs forever. In [16] Alan Turing proved in 1936 that there exists no algorithm, which is able to solve this problem. The Halting Problem can be generalized to Rice's Theorem [17]. Rice's Theorem states, there exists no general method able to decide for any algorithm, if it fulfills a certain non-trivial behavior or not.

Though these problems exist, there is still enough space for software analysis in practice. Therefore, several strategies have been established in order to overcome these limitations:

1. Restrict the problem to a finite state space, only.

2. Use of approximation techniques to gain decidability.

3. A combination of point 1. and 2.

These workarounds lead to current techniques used in software analysis, which are:

1) Abstract Interpretation, 2) Data Flow Analysis, 3) Model Checking, and 4) Theorem Proving.

2.4.1 Abstract Interpretation

In the approach of Abstract Interpretation [18] the concrete semantics of a program is mapped to an abstract semantics. In case this abstraction is sound, the result of an analysis of the abstraction also holds in the concrete representation. In addition the analysis of the abstraction might be easier to compute.

An intuitive example showing the rule of signs is given in [19], which is illustrated in the following. Let $(-1515) * 17$ be an instruction. From this instruction the abstraction to the domain of signs $\{+, -\}$ can be derived. The abstract operations $*$ and $-$ for the abstract values $+$ and $-$ are as follows:

$$-(+) * (+) \Rightarrow (-) * (+) \Rightarrow (-).$$

This leads to the conclusion that $-1515 * 17$ will be a negative number without computing its exact value.

The biggest advantage of the abstraction technique is that due to the abstraction, which usually decreases the complexity of the system to be analyzed, it allows very large systems to be verified. However, the biggest drawback of this approach is that with an increasing level of abstraction a loss in precision comes along. This imprecision raises the risk for possible false positive reports.

2.4.2 Data Flow Analysis

Data Flow Analysis (DFA) [20] is an approach to gather information on the possible set of values in a program. Therefore, the Control Flow Graph (CFG) is analyzed on those paths, where the chosen variable occurs.

A common example for DFA is constant propagation [21, 22, 23], which is used in almost any compiler at a certain optimization level.

2.4.3 Model Checking

In Model Checking (MC) [24, 25] a model – e. g., representing a software program – is checked for a certain property. A common internal representation of this model is a Finite State Machine (FSM).

Since the analysis of programs includes nested structures like loops, recursive function calls, and so on, which may lead to unbounded execution paths, the problem of deriving a suitable model from a given program code exists. The concept of Bounded Model Checking addresses this problem.

Bounded Model Checking

Bounded Model Checking (BMC) [26] is the iterative process, in which a finite approximation of a model – defined over a fixed execution depth – is checked whether it satisfies a certain property or not. The process of iteratively checking model approximations and, in case no violation of the property is found, increased execution depths, is running until either the property holds in one iteration, or the maximum depth is reached.

There exist several formal approaches in model checking in order to prove the correctness of a model with respect to a property. Commonly, a model is given in some automata theoretic notion, i. e., a discrete state transition system, and the property to be checked is formulated in some logic. Starting from this setting there are two main streams of model checking: automata oriented and logic oriented approaches. In the former, the property is translated into an automaton accepting the complement of the language defined by the property. The MC problem is then solved by testing the emptiness of the Cartesian product of the two automata. In case the product is not empty, the model violates the property. In the logic oriented approach, the model is formulated in the logic of the property. Here, the MC problem amounts to the satisfiability problem of the conjunction of the model and the negation of the property formulas. The focus in this work is on the logic oriented approach, in particular, the use of a decision procedure for the satisfiability problem for propositional logic (SAT Solving) or related fragments of first order predicate logic (SMT Solving), which are both introduced in Section 2.5.

2.4.4 Automated Theorem Proving

Automated Theorem Proving (ATP) [27] defines a technique to prove mathematical theorems by using computer programs. Although modern theorem provers are quite powerful, they require human interaction in general and proving/disproving theorems in their logic is usually undecidable. The ATP approach is therefore prohibitively expensive for practical software verification purposes in general.

2.5 The Satisfiability Problem for Propositional Logic

The Satisfiability (SAT) Problem [28, 29] decides for a formula Φ in propositional logic, whether there exists an assignment ψ satisfying Φ or not. This problem is decidable, although computational complex since it is NP complete. A decision procedure for the SAT problem is called SAT-Solver. Such SAT-Solvers usually work either in a probabilistic or deterministic way. Probabilistic SAT-Solvers search for a satisfying assignment by guessing truth values for variables. Empirically, they perform well on randomly generated problems, but not so well on structured problems, like those that occur in the context of software verification. Deterministic SAT-Solvers, however, are more suitable for solving structured SAT problems and are therefore considered here.

The most common form of such a formula Φ is the conjunctive normal form (CNF).

Conjunctive Normal Form

The conjunctive normal form (CNF) is a conjunction of clauses, where a clause consists either of one literal or the disjunction of several literals. A literal denotes either the positive or negative representation of a Boolean variable.

A special type of CNF is the Horn formula. Here, the formula itself is also defined as the conjunction of several Horn clauses. But a Horn clause differs from a common clause in CNF. It is defined as the disjunction of at least one negative literal, but including at most one positive literal.

2.5.1 SAT-Solver

A SAT-Solver is a tool, which given an input formula Φ automatically searches for a solution satisfying Φ. The basic algorithm of almost any common SAT-Solver was established in [30, 31] back in the years 1960-1962 by M. Davis, G. Logemann, D. Loveland and H. Putnam. This is the so-called DPLL algorithm, which is illustrated in Listing 2.2.

Based on this algorithm – including several improvements – the SAT standard [32] has been introduced in the year 2001. The input to such solvers is a formula in CNF.

2. Foundations

Listing 2.2. DPLL Algorithm

```
function DPLL(Φ)
    if all clauses in Φ are satisfied
        return Φ = SAT
    if one clause is unsatisfiable
        return Φ = UNSAT
    for each unitclause c ∈ Φ
        Φ = propagate(c,Φ)
    for each pure literal l ∈ Φ
        Φ = assign(l,Φ)
    l = nextLiteral(Φ)
    return DPLL(Φ ∧ l) ∨ DPLL(Φ ∧ ¬l)
```

Satisfiability of a Formula in CNF

Given a formula in CNF: $\Phi = \bigwedge\limits_{1 \leqslant i \leqslant n} c_i$, where $c_i = \bigvee\limits_{1 \leqslant j \leqslant m} l_j$. An assignment ψ satisfies Φ if the following holds:

$$\psi \models \Phi \Leftrightarrow (\forall c_i : 1 \leqslant i \leqslant n | \exists l_j : 1 \leqslant j \leqslant m : \psi(l_j) = \text{true})$$

Due to the conjunction of clauses, each clause must be fulfilled. Hence, there must exist at least one literal per clause, which is fulfilled.

This leads to the definition of unit propagation, which is a vital part in all state of the art solvers. A clause is called unit in some partial assignment ψ, if it contains only one literal, which has not yet been assigned a truth value, or all literals but one are not true under the assignment ψ. In a satisfying assignment for the formula Φ, the remaining literal must be evaluated as true.

Unit Propagation

In unit propagation the value of the remaining literal of a unit clause, is propagated over the entire set of clauses in the formula Φ. This propagation might lead to a new set of unit clauses, which then also have to be fulfilled. The process runs until either no further unit propagations are possible, or there exists a clause, which cannot be satisfied under the current partial assignment.

There exist approaches where SAT-Solvers are used in software analysis, but since pure SAT only allows Boolean variables, a lot of abstraction is required, which directly leads to possible imprecision. However, the SAT problem can be extended to the so-called Satisfiability Modulo Theories problem.

2.5.2 The Satisfiability Modulo Theories Problem

Commonly, the Satisfiability Modulo Theories (SMT) [33] problem, denotes the satisfiability problems for quantifier free fragments of first order logic, i. e., propositional formulas with predicates instead of propositional variables. The propositional logic is extended by various theories, like e. g., the theory of linear integer arithmetic or the theory of reals. There exists a standard library the Satisfiability Modulo Theories Library (SMT-LIB) [34], which is a database and reference for any common theory in SMT. The two theories of arrays and bit-vectors are particularly interesting for software verification, since the combination of these two can be used to represent memory in computers. Some Model Checking tools like ESBMC [35] and LLBMC [36], which are going to be introduced in Section 2.7, use SMT-Solvers as logical backends dealing with those theories.

2.5.3 Interval Constraint Satisfaction Problem

The Interval Constraint Satisfaction Problem (ICSP) [37] is a special category of the general Constraint Satisfaction Problem (CSP) [38, 39, 40]. The general CSP is defined for a set of constraints C containing a fixed number of variables V. The aim of the CSP is to obtain a set of assignments for the variables in V, which satisfies the restrictions defined by the constraints in C. The ICSP is defined for variables of type real or in general variables, which can be defined over intervals.

A very interesting approach in the ICSP domain resulted in the Interval Constraint Solver HySAT [41] and its successor iSAT. In this approach ICSP and propositional SAT have been merged for the purpose to validate hybrid systems. Therefore, the DPLL algorithm has been extended towards interval constraint propagation. In [42] HySAT was used as an early backend for the verification of common runtime errors. This approach performed quite well, when using simple benchmarks for the proof of concept. Although on bigger benchmarks – with only several hundred lines of code – it did not scale any more. The main bottleneck in this approach had been the logical representation of the physical memory in combination with the unrolling procedure of HySAT. In HySAT the entire model is transformed into a logical formula for each iteration. Therefore, also the memory representation inside the model has to be transformed in each step, resulting in a huge model.

2.6 Compiler Infrastructure

The compiler infrastructure [43, 44] is a framework with which the source code of a program can be transformed into an executable binary. In general such an infrastructure is built on the combination of a Frontend, a Middleend and a Backend. The Frontend of a compiler framework transforms the input source code into the internal intermediate representation – the language model. In the Middleend – depending on the configuration – several optimizations can be applied like e. g., optimization for runtime, resource usage, and so on. The Backend is then used to generate the actual executable for a specific target machine.

2.6.1 Low Level Virtual Machine – LLVM

The "Low Level Virtual Machine" (LLVM) [45] is a compiler infrastructure, which has become more and more popular over the last few years. The heart of LLVM is its intermediate representation, which is going to be introduced in Subsection 2.6.1.1. Figure 2.3 shows the overall workflow of LLVM.

The frontend of LLVM is its actual compiler engine – CLANG [46]. It transforms the input source code, supporting the programming languages C, C++ and Objective-C, into the LLVM intermediate representation. Clang however, is actually a stand-alone compiler, which has the middle- and backend integrated.

2.6.1.1 LLVM Intermediate Representation (IR)

The intermediate representation (IR) [47] of LLVM consists of two parts: 1) The Virtual Instruction Set and 2) The Type System. The virtual machine behind these

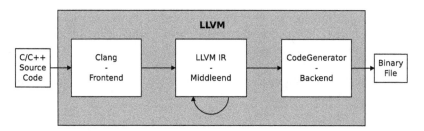

Figure 2.3. The Workflow of LLVM: From Source-Code towards Binary Machine-Code

two is based on MIPS [48] – a RISC computer architecture, which is introduced in Section 2.6.2. The root representation of the C/C++ source code inside the LLVM IR is the LLVM::Module. The module defines the data layout of the chosen target. This includes the type of endianess, as well as the alignment of data for all basic types according to its specific bit widths. In addition the module contains the entire list of global variables. The LLVM::Function represents an actual function of the source code. Inside an LLVM:Module all functions are stored in a list. Each function has a specified return value and a fixed number of arguments. A function is divided into several LLVM::BasisBlocks. The basic block is a sequence of instructions inside LLVM, where the last instruction is either a branch instruction or a terminator instruction.

The Virtual Instruction Set

The LLVM Virtual Instruction Set is based on the MIPS assembly language. Instead of a fixed register set, the LLVM virtual machine is working on an infinite set of virtual registers. The reason therefor is the need for a unique specification, which is consistent over all instructions. This unique specification is called static single assignment form.

Static Single Assignment From

In static single assignment (SSA) [49, 50] form each variable must only be assigned once. This ensures a uniqueness of the value of each variable. Therefore, each variable of a statement is extended by an index. In case variable assign-

2. Foundations

ments are not unique due to branches, so-called phi functions (nodes) are introduced. The phi function determines, which value a variable must have, according to the chosen branch.

In Table 2.5 an example for the transformation of some C statements into SSA form is shown.

Table 2.5. An Example for the Transformation of C Statements into Static Single Assignment Form

	Original C-Statement	SSA Statement
1.	x = x * (y - z);	$x_1 = x_0 * (y_0 - z_0)$;
2.	if (z != 0)	if (z_0 != 0)
3.	x = m / z;	$x_2 = m_0 / z_0$;
4.	else	else
5.	x = 0;	$x_3 = 0$;
6.	n = x * 2t	$x_4 = \phi(x_2, x_3)$; $n_0 = x_4 * 2t$

The Type System

The type system of LLVM is independent of the input source language. It features the common types: void, bool, integers of type signed and unsigned with a bit-width from 8 to 64, as well as single and double precision floating point values. Although LLVM is based on an assembly like language, it still features high-level types, like e. g., arrays, bit vectors and structures.

2.6.1 Example (LLVM IR).
Listing 2.3 shows the LLVM IR for the function worker1 from the previous Example 2.3.1. The function is, as aforementioned, divided into several basic blocks. These blocks are labeled: entry, for.cond, for.body, for.inc, and for.end. In the first block, the corresponding ready signal (worker1Ready) of the function is cleared and the function waits for the signal data1Ready. The block terminates with an unconditional branch into the block for.cond. In this block the loop condition is evaluated and depending on the result, the next branch is

either for.body or for.end. The actual computation of the Laplace operator resides inside the block for.body. This block branches without any condition into the block for.inc. In this block the loop counter is incremented and it terminates with a branch towards for.cond. Inside the last block for.end the signal worker1Ready is triggered and it terminates with the return of type void.

Listing 2.3. The LLVM Intermediate Representation for the Function worker1() of Example 2.3.1.

```
1   define void @worker1() nounwind {
2   entry:
3     %i = alloca i32, align 4
4     %range = alloca i32, align 4
5     call void @clearEvent(i32* @worker1Ready)
6     %0 = load i32* @data1Ready, align 4
7     call void @waintOnEvent(i32 %0)
8     store i32 0, i32* %i, align 4
9     store i32 10, i32* %range, align 4
10    br label %for.cond
11
12  for.cond:
13    %1 = load i32* %i, align 4
14    %2 = load i32* %range, align 4
15    %cmp = icmp slt i32 %1, %2
16    br i1 %cmp, label %for.body, label %for.end
17
18  for.body:
19    %3 = load i32* %i, align 4
20    %call1 = call i32 @left(i32 %3, i32 20)
21    %arrayidx = getelementptr inbounds [20 x i32]* @sensors,
22                i32 0, i32 %call1
23    %4 = load i32* %arrayidx, align 4
24    %5 = load i32* %i, align 4
25    %arrayidx2 = getelementptr inbounds [20 x i32]* @sensors,
26                i32 0, i32 %5
27    %6 = load i32* %arrayidx2, align 4
```

```
28 | %mul = mul nsw i32 2, %6
29 | %sub = sub nsw i32 %4, %mul
30 | %7 = load i32* %i, align 4
31 | %call3 = call i32 @right(i32 %7, i32 20)
32 | %arrayidx4 = getelementptr inbounds [20 x i32]* @sensors,
33 |               i32 0, i32 %call3
34 | %8 = load i32* %arrayidx4, align 4
35 | %add = add nsw i32 %sub, %8
36 | %9 = load i32* %i, align 4
37 | %arrayidx5 = getelementptr inbounds [20 x i32]* @tmp,
38 |               i32 0, i32 %9
39 | store i32 %add, i32* %arrayidx5, align 4
40 | br label %for.inc
41 |
42 | for.inc:
43 |   %10 = load i32* %i, align 4
44 |   %inc = add nsw i32 %10, 1
45 |   store i32 %inc, i32* %i, align 4
46 |   br label %for.cond
47 |
48 | for.end:
49 |   call void @triggerEvent(i32* @worker1Ready)
50 |   ret void
51 | }
```

Although LLVM is based on an assembly language, the fact it still features high-level types like arrays, phi-nodes, pointers, and so on, raises some challenges when it comes to software analysis.

2.6.2 MIPS Assembly

The MIPS [48] architecture is part of the RISC [51] family and widely used in the field of embedded systems. RISC – Reduced Instruction Set Computer – is one of two possible design "philosophies" of micro-processors. Contrary to the CISC [52] family – Complex Instruction Set Computer –, the instruction set featured in RISC is quite small and simple. This lends itself for pipelining and allows high cycle rates. On the other hand, due to the simple chip design the RISC chips are usually cheaper. This fact is important, when it comes to the evaluation of the product cost.

Compared to LLVM, MIPS only features the basic types signed- and unsigned-integer, as well as single- and double-precision floating point. Hence, the difficulties in handling the high-level LLVM type system do not exist.

2.6.2 Example (MIPS Assembly Code of Example 2.3.1).
Listing 2.4 shows the function worker1 of Example 2.3.1 transformed into the MIPS assembly language. Since LLVM is based on MIPS the LLVM IR shown in Listing 2.3 does not differ much from the actual assembly code. The basic block structure is still valid in Listing 2.4. But the need for handling pointers differently from other values is gone, entirely.

Listing 2.4. MIPS Assembly Code of the Function worker1 from Example 2.3.1

```
 1  worker1
 2        .set   noreorder
 3        .set   nomacro
 4
 5  #BB7_0                          # %entry
 6        addiu $sp, $sp, -56
 7        sw    $ra, 52($sp)
 8        addiu $2, $gp, %got(worker1Ready)
 9        addiu $3, $gp, %got(data1Ready)
10        lw    $4, 0($2)
11        lw    $2, 0($3)
12        sw    $2, 40($sp)
13        jal   clearEvent
14        nop
15        lw    $2, 40($sp)
16        lw    $4, 0($2)
17        jal   waitOnEvent
18        nop
```

```
19        addiu $3, $zero, 2
20        sw    $zero, 48($sp)
21        sw    $3, 44($sp)
22        sw    $2, 36($sp)
23
24  $BB7_1                         # %for.cond
25        lw    $2, 48($sp)
26        lw    $3, 44($sp)
27        slt   $2, $2, $3
28        beq   $2, $zero, $BB7_4
29        nop
30        j     $BB7_2
31        nop
32
33  $BB7_2                         # %for.body
34        lw    $4, 48($sp)
35        addiu $2, $zero, 4
36        addu  $5, $zero, $2
37        sw    $2, 32($sp)
38        jal   left
39        nop
40        addiu $4, $gp, %got(sensors)
41        lw    $5, 48($sp)
42        sll   $2, $2, 2
43        lw    $4, 0($4)
44        sll   $3, $5, 2
45        addu  $2, $4, $2
46        addu  $3, $4, $3
47        lw    $3, 0($3)
48        lw    $2, 0($2)
49        sw    $4, 28($sp)
50        addu  $4, $zero, $5
51        lw    $5, 32($sp)
52        sw    $2, 24($sp)
53        sw    $3, 20($sp)
```

```
54          jal    right
55          nop
56          sll    $2, $2, 2
57          lw     $3, 20($sp)
58          sll    $3, $3, 1
59          addiu  $4, $gp, %got(tmp)
60          lw     $5, 28($sp)
61          addu   $2, $5, $2
62          lw     $6, 48($sp)
63          lw     $2, 0($2)
64          lw     $7, 24($sp)
65          subu   $3, $7, $3
66          lw     $4, 0($4)
67          sll    $6, $6, 2
68          addu   $2, $3, $2
69          addu   $3, $4, $6
70          sw     $2, 0($3)
71
72  #BB7_3                          # %for.inc
73          lw     $2, 48($sp)
74          addiu  $2, $2, 1
75          sw     $2, 48($sp)
76          j      $BB7_1
77          nop
78
79  $BB7_4                          # %for.end
80          addiu  $2, $gp, %got(worker1Ready)
81          lw     $4, 0($2)
82          jal    triggerEvent
83          nop
84          lw     $ra, 52($sp)
85          addiu  $sp, $sp, 56
86          jr     $ra
87          nop
```

The sequence for the calculation of the address data1Ready in the first basic block is a good example for showing the differences between the LLVM IR and MIPS assembly, as shown in Table 2.6. The LLVM IR representation is only one single instruction, whereas in MIPS assembly five instructions are required. In the first instruction the global memory address of data1Ready is retrieved from the MIPS internal global offset table (got) and assigned to register $2. The second instruction loads the actual memory position into register $2. In the next step this memory position is stored into the function local stack, since the assembly instruction in line 13 leads to a jump into the function clearEvent. After the return from this call, the next instruction reloads the memory position into register $2. And finally the actual value of data1Ready is assigned to register $4. At first sight the LLVM IR looks much more efficient, but the MIPS assembly represents the "real world". In case of sequential execution, the LLVM IR might be sufficient to detect runtime errors. A tool working directly on the LLVM IR however, in case of concurrent execution, cannot identify all kind of concurrent runtime errors, because not all possible interleavings are considered.

Table 2.6. LLVM IR vs MIPS assembly: Differences between the two Representations of Source Code.

Line	LLVM IR	Line	MIPS Assembly
		9	addiu $3, $gp, %got(data1Ready)
		11	lw $2, 0($3)
6	%0 = load i32* @data1Ready, align 4	12	sw $2, 40($sp)
		15	lw $2, 40($sp)
		16	lw $4, 0($2)

2.7 Related Work

This section introduces related software analysis tools. The main focus is on the techniques used in these approaches, including a short description of the corresponding workflow. In addition, a list of the supported runtime errors which are analyzed is given. Please note, since these lists are based on the corresponding author's (authors') tool publications, the lists might not be complete nor entirely correct.

2.7.1 Blast

The Berkeley Lazy Abstraction Software Verification Tool BLAST [53] was first introduced in 2002. It works based on model checking combined with the counter example guided abstraction refinement (CEGAR) [54] approach. The abstraction techniques used in BLAST are the so-called lazy predicate abstraction [55] and interpolation-based predicate discovery [56]. In this case the term predicate is used for a path condition.

The workflow of the main algorithm in BLAST is illustrated in the following:

1. Transformation of the source code into internal control flow automata (CFA), one for each function.

2. Construction of abstract reachability trees (ART) – based on the CFA –, where the reachability of a node is denoted by the set of constraints on the current path.

3. CEGAR analysis, which checks the feasibility of an error path:

   (a) Path is feasible ⇒ an error has been identified, or

   (b) path is not feasible, start predicate discovery.

4. Predicate discovery is used to find refinement predicates in order to eliminate infeasible errors from the ART(s).

5. Refinement of the ART(s), according to the generated predicates from 4.

6. Continue at 3.

Due to the abstraction, BLAST is able to handle programs with around 50000 lines of code.

Covered Runtime Errors

Since BLAST was designed as a general purpose model checker, there are no common C/C++ runtime errors hard encoded, although the basic checks implemented in BLAST are:

▷ reachability checking

2. Foundations

▷ assertion checking

▷ temporal safety specifications

Limitations

Some of the functions in BLAST may be uninterpreted, which can lead to imprecision in the analysis results. In case of runtime error coverage, BLAST does not
support the check for integer overflows. BLAST has no support for task-based
OS like AUTOSAR/OSEK.

2.7.2 CBMC

CBMC – Bounded Model Checking for ANSI-C – [57] is a software analysis tool,
which was introduced in 2004. The early versions of CBMC used pure SAT-
logic and MINISAT [58] as the corresponding backend solver. Since 2009 CBMC
supports the bit-vector theory of the SMT-Lib, with the backend SMT-Solvers:
Boolector [59], MathSAT [60], and Z3 [61].

The workflow of the main procedure of CBMC is defined as:

1. Preprocessing of the input source code.

2. Transformation and replacement of C statements –like e. g., loops, recursive
   functions, etc. – into suitable representations (for details refer to Section 2.1
   of [57])

3. Generation of a logic formula.

4. Conversion of this formula into CNF, by adding auxiliary variables.

5. Pass the formula to the SMT-Solver and check it for Satisfiability.

Covered Runtime Errors

CBMC can detect the following runtime errors:

▷ array bounds

▷ division by zero

▷ pointer safety

▷ signed/unsigned over- and underflows

▷ floating point NaN check

▷ reachability checking

▷ assertion checking

Limitations

CBMC has no support for task-based OS like AUTOSAR/OSEK.

2.7.3 SATABS

The SATABS [62] software analysis tool, is embedded into the GUI of CBMC. SATABS is the first approach to support ANSI-C fundamentals like arrays and unions. In addition to simple BMC like in CBMC, SATABS is working based on predicate abstraction and refinement.

The main workflow of SATABS is described in the following:

1. Generation of an abstract model by usage of SAT-based Boolean quantification, as described in [63].

2. Transformation of the formula defining this model into CNF.

3. It passes the abstract model to one of the supported backend model checkers: e. g., MOPED [64], SPIN [65], or NuSMV [66].

4. In case the model checker returns a counterexample, SATABS has to check, whether it is spurious, or not. Therefore, it generates a SAT instance for the counterexample and checks it for satisfiability:

   (a) In case of satisfiability $\rightarrow$ SATABS can return an error trace.

   (b) Otherwise, the abstract model has to be refined, and the process continues.

For in depth details on this workflow, please see [62, 67, 68, 69].

2. Foundations

Covered Runtime Errors

SATABS can detect the following runtime errors:

▷ array bounds (buffer overflows)

▷ pointer safety

▷ exceptions

▷ control-flow oriented user-specified assertions.

Limitations

SATABS does not support task-based OS like AUTOSAR/OSEK.

2.7.4 ESBMC

The ESBMC [35] software analysis tool was introduced in 2009. ESBMC is basically built on the base of CBMC to generate the properties to verify. However, ESBMC has extended CBMC to use more SMT theories as in the original approach. In addition, ESBMC features a primitive scheduling model in order to handle POSIX threads. ESMBC is supporting the two SMT-Solvers Boolector and Z3.

The workflow of ESBMC is described in the following:

1. CBMC preprocessing until step 4. as described in Section 2.7.2.

2. Choose the selected SMT-Solver.

3. Derive the logic formula via conversion of the CBMC constraints and properties.

4. Pass the formula to the SMT-Solver and check it for Satisfiability.

In case of concurrent analysis for POSIX, ESBMC is generating a reachability tree and checking all possible interleavings in this tree.

Covered Runtime Errors

ESBMC can detect the following runtime errors:

▷ arithmetic under- and overflow

▷ pointer safety

▷ memory leaks

▷ array bounds

▷ atomicity and order violations

▷ deadlock

▷ data race

Limitations

ESMBC has no support for task-based OS like AUTOSAR/OSEK.

2.7.5 LLBMC

LLBMC [36], the Low Level Bounded Model Checker is a software analysis tool, which is working on LLVM. The verification Backends used in LLBMC are the SMT-Solver Boolector, working on the SMT-Lib category bit-vector, and the SMT-Solver STP [70], a constraint solver for program analysis tools.

The main workflow of LLBMC is the following:

1. Compilation of the input source code into the LLVM IR.

2. Generate SMT logic formulas based on the LLVM IR, containing:

   (a) The entire memory management, and

   (b) all assumptions about possible errors.

3. Let the logical backend check if any of the error assumptions holds.

2. Foundations

Covered Runtime Errors

LLBMC can detect the following runtime errors:

▷ Integer overflow

▷ Division by zero

▷ Invalid bit shift

▷ Illegal memory access (array index out of bound, illegal pointer access, etc.)

▷ Invalid free

▷ Double free

▷ User-customizable checks (via __llbmc_assume / __llbmc_assert)

Limitations

Though LLBMC supports the entire C language family, it does not feature floating point types. Moreover LLBMC does not support a task-based OS like AUTOSAR/OSEK. In addition, there are currently no checks for concurrent issues available.

2.7.6 Predator

Predator [71] has been introduced in 2011. It is a software analysis tool, built for the verification of sequential C code, with a specialization on dynamic linked data structure. In the first version, Predator used separation logic in combination with inductive predicates. Later, the separation logic was replaced by a graph-based representation in order to benefit from the massive set of graph-based algorithms. The latest redesign of its internal representation lead to symbolic memory graphs (SMGs).

The overall workflow of Predator is described in the following:

1. Creation of a Control Flow Graph (CFG) for the input C code.

2. Iterative generation of sets of SMGs for all basic blocks of the CFG.

3. Analyze the SMGs with the help of an abstraction- and a join-algorithm. For details on these two algorithms see [72].

4. In case of no error and not all configurations have been checked, go to 2.

Covered Runtime Errors

Predator is – according to the authors – able to detect the following runtime errors:

▷ null dereferences

▷ double deletion

▷ memory leakage

Limitations

As aforementioned, Predator is built for sequential C code and is therefore not able to identify critical race conditions. This also means that Predator is not able to handle task-based OS like AUTOSAR/OSEK. In addition it also does not seem to be able to handle arithmetic runtime errors, like e. g., a division by zero.

2.7.7 Threader

The software analysis tool Threader [73] has been introduced in 2011. The main purpose of Threader is the verification of multi-threaded programs. It is working according to the CEGAR [54] technique. Threader uses the CIL framework [74] to generate its internal transition system including specific properties, which defines constraints over the shared variables in the program.

The workflow of Threader is described in the following:

1. Generation of the internal transition system via CIL.

2. Check the transition system for the reachability of an error state.

   (a) In case no error state is reachable → Abstraction is safe.

   (b) Otherwise, generate a set of Horn clauses representing the path to the error.

3. Pass Horn clauses to Horn-Solver and check for Satisfiability:

   (a) In case the clauses are satisfiable → error has been found (including counterexample)

   (b) Otherwise, candidate was a false-positive → refinement of the abstraction model

4. Continue with 2.

Covered Runtime Errors

Threader is able to verify multi-threaded programs. From the documentation it decides over the reachability of either assertions or specified error-labels.

Limitations

There is no support for recursive functions, since Threader's preprocessing engine uses function inlining. Though Threader supports concurrent programs, it does not feature task-based OS like AUTOSAR/OSEK. In addition it seems that threader is not supporting the detection of critical race conditions.

2.8 Related Industrial Tools

This section introduces the three industrial static analysis tools: Astrée, Bauhaus and Polyspace, which are working based on abstract interpretation and pattern matching.

2.8.1 Astrée

The Astrée analyzer [75, 76, 77, 78] was introduced in 2003 at the Laboratoire d'Informatique of the École Normale Supérieur. Astrée is a static software analysis tool, which is working based on abstract interpretation. For details on those abstraction techniques, please refer to [78]. The workflow of Astrée is described in the following:

1. Generation of the intermediate representation by a compiler-like front-end.

2. Independent analysis in order to gather relevant informations, e. g., variable dependencies.

3. Generation of invariants based on the criteria assembled in step 2.

4. Checking of the invariants using several abstract domains [79] and error reporting.

Though this description looks quite easy, Astrée features many different options, which all must be manually enabled and most of them require advanced knowledge.

2.8.2 Bauhaus

The Bauhaus [80] Tool Suite is a combination of several functionalities, where the main purpose is to cover and guide the entire development process. In order to analyze large or even huge industrial projects, the implemented features are working based on approximative techniques. This can lead to large numbers of false positive reports, which have to be checked by a manual review. The features covered by Bauhaus are:

▷ architectural checks

▷ code clone detection

▷ code style checks (Misra C/C++ [81])

▷ several code metrics

▷ dead code detection

▷ and many more

In addition there exists experimental work for the detection of data races [82].

2.8.3 Polyspace

Polyspace [83] is a static software analysis tool for C/C++ source code of the Mathworks group. The latest version of Polyspace is actually divided into two tools: the Polyspace Bug Finder™and the Polyspace Code Prover™. The first one is a basic static software analysis tool, which is able to identify several runtime errors. A detailed list of runtime errors can be found on the Polyspace website. The second one is using abstract interpretation and also static analysis to prove the absence of the runtime errors: like e. g., overflow, division by zero, out-of-bounds array access.

Though Polyspace is able to handle a large amount of source code, it still produces error candidates, which it cannot verify. These candidates have to be checked in a manual review.

Although some of the academic software analysis tools are already capable of handling concurrent software, none of them is able to identify race conditions in an automotive system based on AUTOSAR or OSEK. On the other hand, the industrial tool Bauhaus is in its experimental race detection engine able to tackle this problem, but the amount of resulting error candidates is too big for a manual review.

Chapter 3

The MEMICS Software Verification Approach

The Memory Interval Constraint Solving (MEMICS) [84, 85, 86] software verification approach is able to detect a wide range of runtime errors in C/C++ software from a division by zero up to critical race conditions. In Figure 3.1 the architectural overview of MEMICS is illustrated.

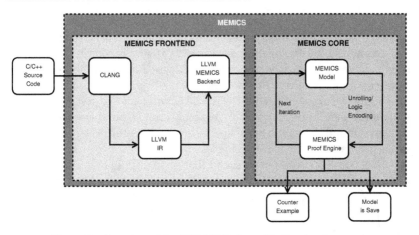

Figure 3.1. Overview of the MEMICS Software Verification Approach

In the first step of the process, MEMICS transforms the source code using the LLVM compiler infrastructure into its own model. In the actual verification process the internal model is unrolled step by step and transformed into a logic formula in SSA form. This formula is then passed to the solver of MEMICS, which checks, whether the formula and respectively the underlying software suffers from any runtime error. The process continues until: the entire source code is proven to be free of any runtime error, an error is detected or a timeout occurred. Please note that the current focus of runtime error detection in MEMICS is on those listed in Table 2.3, although the general approach can easily be extended by other error categories.

The main focus of MEMICS is the identification of runtime errors in automotive software, in particular the detection and/or verification of critical race conditions. This is of high relevance, since the introduction of multicore hardware to the automotive domain greatly increases the risk for potential race conditions.

3.1 The MEMICS Frontend

The MEMICS Frontend generates the MEMICS Model from the input C/C++ source code. This generation process, shown in Figure 3.2, is embedded into the LLVM compiler infrastructure. For details on LLVM, see Section 2.6.1. The process is split into three different steps. First, CLANG is used to compile the input C/C++ source code into the LLVM IR. Please note that all optimizations are disabled in the compile process per default. The reason is, compiler optimizations are used to optimize the executable code, like e. g., for runtime. But these optimizations can have an impact on the behavior of the software itself. The last step is the actual generation of the MEMICS Model.

In Section 2.6.1 it has been stated that, though the LLVM IR is based on MIPS assembly, it still contains high-level language features, like e. g., pointers. The MEMICS Model, which is introduced in detail in Section 3.2, is built based directly on MIPS assembly. In order to properly generate this model out of the LLVM IR, a new target code generating backend has been embedded into LLVM. This backend is built based on the MIPS backend of LLVM, with some minor modifications in the target specific lowering rules. Also, instead of creating a plain assembly instruction, the backend builds a MEMICS instruction – as defined in Section 3.2.3 – and adds it to the model.

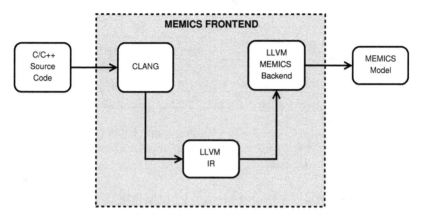

Figure 3.2. Overview of the Frontend of the MEMICS Software Verification Approach

3.2 The MEMICS Model

The MEMICS Model is defined as a finite state machine $M = <S, T>$, with a set of states $S = \{s_1, \ldots, s_n\}$ and a set of transitions $T = \{t_1, \ldots, t_m\}$. A transition $t_i \in T$ is defined as a 4-tuple: $< s_i, a, c, s_i' >$, where s_i describes the current state of the model, a is the actual action of a MIPS instruction, c is an optional condition - e. g., required for branch instructions - and s_i' is the successor state of the model. The four general MEMICS instructions types are shown in Table 3.1.

Table 3.1. Logic Representation of the four General Instruction Types inside the MEMICS Model.

Instruction Type	Logic Definition	Description
basic	$s_i \rightarrow a \wedge s_i'$	*The current state s_i implies the execution of instruction a and the successor state s_i'.*
conditional	$s_i \wedge c \rightarrow a \wedge s_i'$	*The current state s_i and the condition c imply the execution of instruction a and the successor state s_i'.*

| conditional jump | $s_i \wedge c \rightarrow s_i'$ | *The current state s_i and the condition c imply the successor state s_i'.* |
| unconditional jump | $s_i \rightarrow s_i'$ | *An unconditional jump, where the current state s_i implies the successor state s_i'.* |

Before the syntax of the MEMICS Model and the entire instruction set can be introduced, the virtual CPU and the corresponding memory modeling inside MEMICS have to be described.

3.2.1 The virtual CPU and Memory of the MEMICS Model

The virtual CPU of the model supports an arbitrary number of processor cores, where each core consists of all the registers featured by the MIPS assembly language. This includes 32 common integer registers in two's complement, e. g., the global pointer, return address and stack pointer registers, as well as 32 floating point registers. Though MEMICS does not require a separate co-processor for floating point operations, all floating point instructions in MEMICS are still in line with the MIPS assembly language. Therefore, the system still has to transfer data between integer and floating point registers, if needed.

The system memory of MEMICS is currently modeled by a byte-sized array of dynamic range. Since the default endianess of the MIPS assembly backend of LLVM is big endian, the current implementation of the memory model featured in MEMICS is big endian, too. The alignment of the memory model is per default configured to four byte. Both, the alignment and the endianess are configurable in order to meet any kind of target architecture required by the user. The maximum size of the modeled memory is configurable. The adjustment of the internal memory is illustrated in Figure 3.3. The first memory block repre-

Figure 3.3. The Memory Adjustment of the internal Memory modeled in MEMICS

sents the global offset table, in which the base addresses of all global variables and functions are stored. The static memory block covers the actual memory location for each global variable. Function local memory - the stack - is placed in the stack memory block. The default stack size of a function can either be computed by the LLVM MEMICS backend or passed to MEMICS via a configuration file. In the last block, all heap memory is dynamically allocated. Initially this block is empty. If MEMICS runs out of memory during a verification run, the corresponding exception is thrown.

3.2.2 Syntax of the MEMICS Model

The syntactical definition of the MEMICS Model – the Intermediate Representation (IR) – is the encoding of a program into the Formula introduced in Table 3.2.

Table 3.2. Syntax of the MEMICS Model

		Model
Formula	::=	Formula ∧ Formula
	‖	Instruction
Instruction	::=	Condition → Action
	‖	Action
	‖	Condition
		Condition
Condition	::=	$\circ_{bool}$(Condition, Condition)
	‖	CondExpr
CondExpr	::=	$\sim_{rel}$ (Reg, Reg)
	‖	Reg
	‖	¬(CondExpr)
		Action
Action	::=	Action ∧ Action
	‖	ActExpr
ActExpr	::=	Reg' := Expr
	‖	$\circ_{load}$(Reg', memAdr(Reg, Reg), Reg)
	‖	$\circ_{store}$(Reg, memAdr(Reg, Reg), Reg)
	‖	memcpy(Reg, Reg, Reg)
	‖	memset(Reg, Reg, Reg)

3. The MEMICS Software Verification Approach

Expr	::=	calloc(Reg, Reg)
‖		$\circ$memory (Reg)
‖		$\circ$binary (Reg, Reg)
‖		$\circ$cast (Reg)
‖		$\circ$unary (Reg)

Operators

$\sim$rel	::=	$\circ$compare_float
‖		$\circ$compare_signed
‖		$\circ$compare_unsigned
$\circ$binary	::=	$\circ$binary_float
‖		$\circ$binary_signed
‖		$\circ$binary_unsigned
‖		$\circ$bit
‖		$\sim$rel
$\circ$bit	::=	and ‖ or ‖ xor ‖ sl ‖ sr
$\circ$bool	::=	$\wedge$ ‖ $\vee$ ‖ $\rightarrow$ ‖ $\leftrightarrow$
$\circ$cast	::=	foat2float ‖ float2int ‖ int2float
‖		int2int
$\circ$load	::=	lb ‖ lbu ‖ lh ‖ lhu ‖ lw ‖ ld
$\circ$memory	::=	malloc ‖ free ‖ new ‖ delete
$\circ$store	::=	sb ‖ sh ‖ sw ‖ sd
$\circ$unary	::=	$\circ$unary_float
‖		$\circ$unary_signed
‖		$\circ$unary_unsigned

Float Operators

$\circ$binary_float	::=	addF ‖ subF ‖ mulF ‖ divF
‖		powF ‖ nrootF ‖ minF ‖ maxF
$\circ$compare_float	::=	eqF ‖ neqF ‖ sltF ‖ sleqF
‖		sgtF ‖ sgeqF
$\circ$unary_float	::=	abF ‖ expF ‖ logF ‖ sqrtF
‖		cosF ‖ sinF ‖ tanF
‖		arccosF ‖ arcsinF ‖ arctanF

Signed Operators		
$\circ_{\text{binary\_signed}}$	::=	add ‖ sub ‖ mul ‖ div
	‖	pow ‖ nroot ‖ min ‖ max
$\circ_{\text{compare\_signed}}$	::=	eq ‖ neq ‖ slt ‖ sleq ‖ sgt ‖ sgeq
$\circ_{\text{unary\_signed}}$	::=	ab ‖ exp ‖ log ‖ sqrt ‖ cos ‖ sin
	‖	tan ‖ arccos ‖ arcsin ‖ arctan
Unsigned Operators		
$\circ_{\text{binary\_unsigned}}$	::=	addU ‖ subU ‖ mulU ‖ divU
	‖	powU ‖ nrootU ‖ minU ‖ maxU
$\circ_{\text{compare\_unsigned}}$	::=	eqU ‖ neqU ‖ sltU ‖ slequ
	‖	sgtU ‖ sgeqU
$\circ_{\text{unary\_unsigned}}$	::=	expU ‖ logU ‖ sqrtU
	‖	cosU ‖ sinU ‖ tanU
	‖	arccosU ‖ arcsinU ‖ arctanU

A Reg represents a register of the internal virtual machine, which has been introduced in Section 3.2.1. Since such a register, which can either be a floating-point register or an integer register, contains a simple bit-vector, the operator itself contains the actual encoding for interpreting its value. Therefore, there exist three different operators: one operator for floating-point operations, one for signed integer operations and one for unsigned integer operations. All the corresponding instructions are introduced in Section 3.2.3. The prime or next operator (′) defines the "next" state of the current register. It is required by MEMICS unrolling procedure, which is introduced in Section 3.4.1, in order to ensure a proper SSA encoding of the formula.

Please note that the operators: bit, binary, compare, and unary can also be represented by their equivalent mathematical symbol, defined as:

$$\circ_{\text{op}}(\text{Reg, Reg}) \equiv (\text{Reg } \circ_{\text{math(op)}} \text{Reg}).$$

E.g., the instruction $a' := \text{add}(b, c)$ is equivalent to the instruction: $a' := b + c$. In case the operator is of type floating-point the mathematical operator must still carry this information, e.g., addF $\equiv$ +F and addU $\equiv$ +U.

3.2.3 The MEMICS Instruction Set

The instruction set of MEMICS is, as aforementioned, based on the MIPS instruction set. This section introduces all instructions covered by MEMICS. The actual instruction, corresponding to an actual machine instruction, is either an assignment or a relation – as shown in Table 3.1 the action a or the condition c. This section is divided into the definitions of the arithmetic instructions (Subsection 3.2.3.1), the memory instructions (Subsection 3.2.3.2), the type relevant instructions (Subsection 3.2.3.3) and the synchronization instructions (Subsection 3.2.3.4).

All of the instructions shown in this section are atomic in the current implementation of MEMICS. Therefore, they are not interruptable.

3.2.3.1 Arithmetic Instructions

The block of arithmetic instructions is the biggest one inside the MEMICS instruction set. Arithmetic wise, MEMICS supports floating point, signed and unsigned integer, as well as bitwise integer instructions. Since the integer registers of a common MIPS machine are in tow's complement, the interpretation of the encoding is directly handled in the instruction. Therefore, the floating point, signed integer and unsigned integer instructions only differ in the interpretation of the value inside a register. Due to this fact, this section only covers the signed integer and bitwise integer instructions. The definitions for floating point and unsigned integer instructions are located in the Appendix in Table B.1 and Table B.2.

The first type of arithmetic instructions – the basic ones – are shown in the first block of Table 3.3. These instructions are: addition, subtraction, multiplication, and division of two corresponding operands. In the second block of this table, the bitwise instructions are shown. This block of instructions covers simple operations like bitwise and, or, and xor. In addition also bitwise shift operations, like right and left shift are supported. In the last block of this table, all the relational instructions featured in MEMICS are shown. These instructions cover all kind of lower and greater relations, as well as the equal and not-equal relation.

Table 3.3. MEMICS Instruction Set: Signed Integer Instructions – Basic Arithmetic, Bitwise and Relational Operations

Instruction	Description
a' := add(b, c);	The result of the addition of registers b and c is stored in register a.
a' := sub(b, c);	The result of the subtraction of registers b and c is stored in register a.
a' := mul(b, c);	The result of the multiplication of registers b and c is stored in register a.
a' := div(b, c);	The result of the division of register b by c is stored in register a.
a' := and(b, c);	The result of the bitwise "and" of registers b and c is stored in register a.
a' := or(b, c);	The result of the bitwise "or" of registers b and c is stored in register a.
a' := xor(b, c);	The result of the bitwise "xor" of registers b and c is stored in register a.
a' := sl(b, c);	The value from register b is shifted to the left by the amount located in the register c and the result is stored in register a.
a' := sr(b, c);	The value from register b is shifted to the right by the amount located in the register c and the result is stored in register a.
a' := sge(b, c);	The result of the greater-equal relation between the registers b and c is stored in register a.
a' := sgt(b, c);	The result of the greater-than relation between the registers b and c is stored in register a.
a' := sle(b, c);	The result of the smaller-equal relation between the registers b and c is stored in register a.
a' := slt(b, c);	The result of the smaller-than relation between the registers b and c is stored in register a.
a' := seq(b, c);	The result of the equal relation between the registers b and c is stored in register a.

$a' := \text{sneq}(b, c);$	The result of the not-equal relation between the registers b and c is stored in register a.

All instructions introduced so far are covered in the MIPS assembly language. Since the Solver in MEMICS is more advanced than a simple assembly machine, the instruction set of MEMICS covers far more arithmetic instructions, which are introduced in the following.

Table 3.4 shows the advanced arithmetic instructions as well as the gradient, sign and relational specific instructions of MEMICS. The first block covers the exponential function, power function, logarithm, square-root and the n-th root. Since none of these functions is directly supported by the MIPS assembly language, either at least a common math header or an additional MEMICS header has to be included. The gradient block features the basic cosine, tangent and sine instructions, as well as their arc version. The sign instruction is covering the absolute value. Whereas the relational instructions feature the minimum as well as the maximum arithmetic for two operands.

Table 3.4. MEMICS Instruction Set: Signed Integer Instructions – Advanced Arithmetic

Instruction	Description
$a' := \exp(b);$	The result of the exponential function applied to register b is stored in register a.
$a' := \text{pow}(b, c);$	The power function of the value from register b to the basis of the value in register c is computed and stored in the register a.
$a' := \log(b);$	The logarithm of the value from register b is computed and stored in register a.
$a' := \text{sqrt}(b);$	The square-root of the value from register b is computed and stored in register a.
$a' := \text{nroot}(b, c);$	The nth-root of the value from register b, where n is defined by register c, is assigned to register a.
$a' := \cos(b);$	The cosine value of the value from register b is stored in register a.
$a' := \tan(b);$	The sine value of the value from register b is stored in register a.

a′ := sin(b);	The tangent value of the value from register b is stored in register a.
a′ := arccos(b);	The arc cosine value of the value from register b is stored in register a.
a′ := arctan(b);	The arc sine value of the value from register b is stored in register a.
a′ := arcsin(b);	The arc tangent value of the value from register b is stored in register a.
a′ := abs(b);	The absolute value of register b is stored in register a.
a′ := min(b, c);	The minimum of the registers b and c is stored in register a.
a′ := max(b, c);	The maximum of the registers b and c is stored in register a.

3.2.3.2 Memory Instructions

MEMICS is the first ICS with an embedded memory model. Therefore, the instruction set features several memory related instructions. In Table 3.5 the instructions for memory allocation and freeing are shown. These allocation and freeing operations access the virtual memory introduced in Section 3.2.1. In case of arrays and structures MEMICS allocates memory regions according to the currently configured alignment. This can vary for different machine types. Therefore, one has to be careful, with direct accesses to such regions, where the access is directly encoded into the operation.

Table 3.5. MEMICS Instruction Set: Memory Management Instructions – Allocation and Freeing

Instruction	Description
a′ := calloc(b, c);	Allocate a number of memory blocks, where the number is defined by the value in register b and the size of each block in register c. The base-address of the entire block is stored in register a.
a′ := malloc(b);	Allocate an amount of bytes defined by the value of the register b and the resulting base-address is stored in register a.

free(a);	Free the memory region starting from the base-address defined by register a. The amount of bytes to free is retrieved via the malloc table.

Table 3.6 shows the MEMICS instructions for copying and setting memory regions. These representatives of the memcpy and memset functions are very useful in order to reduce the complexity of the sources to analyze. Their usage however, can be responsible for the non-detection of race conditions in a concurrent "execution" of e. g., a memcpy operation and a memset operation. Therefore, the user can configure whether he or she wants to use the built-in versions, or not. In case not, he or she also has to provide the sources for these operations, since there exist several different implementations of these operations.

Table 3.6. MEMICS Instruction Set: Memory Management Instructions – Memory Copy, Set and Miscellaneous

Instruction	Description
memcpy(a, b, c);	Copy n bytes from the base-address defined in register b, where n is defined in register c, to the memory region starting at the base-address defined in register a.
memset(a, b, c);	Store b into n bytes – n is defined in register c – from the base-address defined in register a.
a' := memAdr(b, c);	Compute the memory address starting at register b with an offset defined in register c and store it in register a.
memRst(b, c);	Reset the memory region from the address defined in register b for n bytes, defined in register c.
a' := getGlobalIndex(<b>);	Retrieve the base-address of the global variable defined by the identifier <b> and store it in register a.
a' := getJumpIndex(<b>);	Get the program counter index of a function or basic block defined by the identifier <b> and store it in register a.

The memAdr instruction is required by the load- and store-instructions, which are introduced in Table 3.7. This instruction computes a memory address based on a base-address and a corresponding offset. The last instruction in this block is the memRst instruction, which is used for local stack memory management. With this function such local stack regions can be entirely reset and assigned to undefined values.

In Table 3.7 all load and store instructions featured in MEMICS are shown.

Table 3.7. MEMICS Instruction Set: Load and Store Instructions

Instruction	Description
lb(a', memAdr(b, c), _clk_);	Read one byte from the memory address computed by *memAdr* and store it in register a. _clk_ is required for analysis of concurrent errors.
lbu(a', memAdr(b, c), _clk_);	Read one byte from the memory address computed by *memAdr*, interpreted as an unsigned value and store it in register a. _clk_ is required for analysis of concurrent errors.
lh(a', memAdr(b, c), _clk_);	Read two bytes from the memory address computed by *memAdr* and store the result in register a. _clk_ is required for analysis of concurrent errors.
lhu(a', memAdr(b, c), _clk_);	Read two bytes from the memory address computed by *memAdr*, interpreted as unsigned values and store the result in register a. _clk_ is required for analysis of concurrent errors.
lw(a', memAdr(b, c), _clk_);	Four bytes from the memory address computed by *memAdr* and store the result in register a. _clk_ is required for analysis of concurrent errors.

ld(a′, memAdr(b, c), _clk_);	Read eight bytes from the memory address computed by *memAdr* and store the result in register a. _clk_ is required for analysis of concurrent errors.
sb(a, memAdr(b, c), _clk_);	Store the value of register a into one byte at the memory address computed by *memAdr*. _clk_ is required for analysis of concurrent errors.
sh(a, memAdr(b, c), _clk_);	Store the value of register a into two bytes starting at the base-address computed by *memAdr*. _clk_ is required for analysis of concurrent errors.
sw(a, memAdr(b, c), _clk_);	Store the value of register a into four bytes starting at the base-address computed by *memAdr*. _clk_ is required for analysis of concurrent errors.
sd(a, memAdr(b, c), _clk_);	Store the value of register a into eight bytes starting at the base-address computed by *memAdr*. _clk_ is required for analysis of concurrent errors.

Each of these instructions first computes the base address required for the operation. In the next step of a load instruction, the corresponding amount of bytes is read from the memory and finally assembled together. The amount of bytes is directly encoded in the instruction name, from one byte towards eight bytes. The _clk_ is required for the detection of race conditions, which is explained in detail in Section 3.4.6. The store instructions operate analogously to the load instructions, but instead of reading from the memory they store an amount of bytes into a memory region.

3.2.3.3 Cast and Conversion Instructions

Since MEMICS currently works like a MIPS machine regarding floating point instructions, the co-processor directives have to be met. Therefore, MEMICS also features the two move commands, which copy the bit-representation of an integer register into a floating point register and vice versa. These two instructions are shown in Table 3.8. Since the current implementation only features 32-bit long words, these move instructions can copy the bit-vector of one register into the other, immediately.

Table 3.8. MEMICS Instruction Set: Communication between Floating Point and Integer Registers

Instruction	Description
mov_w_f(a, b_{fp});	Copy each bit from register a into the floating point register b_{fp}.
mov_f_w(a_{fp}, b);	Copy each bit from the floating point register a_{fp} into register b.

The actual conversion between an integer bit-vector into its corresponding floating point bit-vector, among floating point bit-vectors and vice versa is handled by a separate set of instructions. These instructions are introduced in Table 3.9. Please note that none of the original assembly instructions feature several rounding modes, whereas MEMICS currently only supports "round to nearest" (RN). In the first block all the instructions converting into double-precision floating point are shown. The source can either be a long-word, single-precision float or a word. The second block features those instructions casting towards a single-precision float, where the sources are the same as for the previous block. In the last block all the instructions covering casts from floating point into either a long-word or word integer representation are shown. The source can either be a single- or double-precision float for both cases.

Table 3.9. MEMICS Instruction Set: Cast Instructions

Instruction	Description
$a' := \text{cvt\_d\_l}(b)$;	Convert the long word from register b into a double precision float and store it in register a.
$a' := \text{cvt\_d\_s}(b)$;	Convert the single precision float from register b into a double precision float and store it in register a.

a' := cvt_d_w(b);	Convert the word from register b into a double precision float and store it in register a.
a' := cvt_s_d(b);	Convert the double precision float from register b into a single precision float and store it in register a.
a' := cvt_s_l(b);	Convert the long word from register b into a single precision float and store it in register a.
a' := cvt_s_w(b);	Convert the word from register b into a single precision float and store it in register a.
a' := cvt_l_d(b);	Convert the double precision float from register b into a long word and store it in register a.
a' := cvt_l_s(b);	Convert the single precision float from register b into a long word and store it in register a.
a' := cvt_w_d(b);	Convert the double precision float from register b into a word and store it in register a.
a' := cvt_w_s(b);	Convert the single precision float from register b into a word and store it in register a.

In Table 3.10 all the round instructions featured in MEMICS are shown. These instructions cover the basic round, truncate, ceil, and floor operations. The rounding criterion for the round instruction is "round to the nearest". The source of the instruction is either a single- or double-precision float and the corresponding destination either a long-word or word integer. The rounding criterion for the truncate instruction is: "round towards zero". For the ceil instruction the criterion is: "round up" and the criterion for the floor instruction is: "round down".

Table 3.10. MEMICS Instruction Set: Round Instructions – Round, Truncate, Ceil and Floor

Instruction	Description
a' := round_l_d(b);	The round value of the double precision floating point value from register b is stored as a long word in register a.
a' := round_l_s(b);	The round value of the single precision floating point value from register b is stored as a long word in register a.

$a' := \text{round\_w\_d}(b);$	The round value of the double precision floating point value from register b is stored as a word in register a.
$a' := \text{round\_w\_s}(b);$	The round value of the single precision floating point value from register b is stored as a word in register a.
$a' := \text{trunc\_l\_d}(b);$	The truncated value of the double precision floating point value from register b is stored as a long word in register a.
$a' := \text{trunc\_l\_s}(b);$	The truncated value of the single precision floating point value from register b is stored as a long word in register a.
$a' := \text{trunc\_w\_d}(b);$	The truncated value of the double precision floating point value from register b is stored as a word in register a.
$a' := \text{trunc\_w\_s}(b);$	The truncated value of the single precision floating point value from register b is stored as a word in register a.
$a' := \text{ceil\_l\_d}(b);$	The ceiled value of the double precision floating point value from register b is stored as a long word in register a.
$a' := \text{ceil\_l\_s}(b);$	The ceiled value of the single precision floating point value from register b is stored as a long word in register a.
$a' := \text{ceil\_w\_d}(b);$	The ceiled value of the double precision floating point value from register b is stored as a word in register a.
$a' := \text{ceil\_w\_s}(b);$	The ceiled value of the single precision floating point value from register b is stored as a word in register a.
$a' := \text{floor\_l\_d}(b);$	The floor value of the double precision floating point value from register b is stored as a long word in register a.
$a' := \text{floor\_l\_s}(b);$	The floor value of the single precision floating point value from register b is stored as a long word in register a.

a' := floor_w_d(b);	The floor value of the double precision floating point value from register b is stored as a word in register a.
a' := floor_w_s(b);	The floor value of the single precision floating point value from register b is stored as a word in register a.

3.2.3.4 Synchronization Instructions

In order to provide a synchronization mechanism, MEMICS features the waitOn-Event instruction, which is introduced in Table 3.11. In the current implementation of MEMICS this mechanism works according to the WaitEvent definition in the OSEK OS specification [6].

Table 3.11. MEMICS Instruction Set: Synchronization Instructions

Instruction	Description
waitOnEvent(a);	This functions checks whether the value of an event, stored in register a, is true or not.

3.2.4 Mapping of C/C++ Source Code

In order to locate errors later on directly in the source code, a mapping between the input code and an instruction inside the model must be achieved. For this purpose the MEMICS assembly backend uses the DWARF [87, 88] debug information, which is already available in LLVM. At each lowering of an assembly instruction to a MEMICS instruction, the backend equips the new instruction with the information on the file name, the location inside the file and the according label, representing the actual C variable behind the location.

3.2.1 Example (The MEMICS Model of the Automotive Race Condition Example 2.3.1).
In Listing 3.1 the MEMICS Model for the function worker1 of the automotive example is shown. The entire model can be found in Appendix A. The structure of the basic blocks is equivalent to those from Listing 2.4, although they are

actually not used in MEMICS. Instead, the program counter (PC) is hard-coded into the model. Since MEMICS is built based directly on the MIPS assembly language, the access to a global variable is equivalent to Example 2.6.2, like e. g., the first access of data1Ready at PC 179.

Listing 3.1. The MEMICS Model of the Function worker1 of the Automotive Race Condition Example

```
1   PC = 174 -> PC' = 175;
2   PC = 175 -> PC' = 176;
3   PC = 176 -> sp_reg' = sp_reg +U 4294967240 AND PC' = 177;
4   PC = 177 -> sw(ra_reg, memAdr(sp_reg, 52), _clk_) AND PC' = 178;
5   PC = 178 -> 2_reg' = gp_reg +U getGlobalIndex(worker1Ready) AND
6               PC' = 179;
7   PC = 179 -> 3_reg' = gp_reg +U getGlobalIndex(data1Ready) AND
8               PC' = 180;
9   PC = 180 -> lw(4_reg', memAdr(2_reg, 0), _clk_) AND PC' = 181;
10  PC = 181 -> lw(2_reg', memAdr(3_reg, 0), _clk_) AND PC' = 182;
11  PC = 182 -> sw(2_reg, memAdr(sp_reg, 40), _clk_) AND PC' = 183;
12  PC = 183 -> ra_reg' = 185 AND PC' = 1;
13  PC = 184 -> PC' = 185;
14  PC = 185 -> lw(2_reg', memAdr(sp_reg, 40), _clk_) AND PC' = 186;
15  PC = 186 -> lw(4_reg', memAdr(2_reg, 0), _clk_) AND PC' = 187;
16  PC = 187 AND waitOnEvent(data1Ready)-> PC' = 188;
17  PC = 188 -> PC' = 189;
18  PC = 189 -> 3_reg' = 0 +U 2 AND PC' = 190;
19  PC = 190 -> sw(0, memAdr(sp_reg, 48), _clk_) AND PC' = 191;
20  PC = 191 -> sw(3_reg, memAdr(sp_reg, 44), _clk_) AND PC' = 192;
21  PC = 192 -> sw(2_reg, memAdr(sp_reg, 36), _clk_) AND PC' = 193;
22  PC = 193 -> lw(2_reg', memAdr(sp_reg, 48), _clk_) AND PC' = 194;
23  PC = 194 -> lw(3_reg', memAdr(sp_reg, 44), _clk_) AND PC' = 195;
24  PC = 195 -> 2_reg' = 2_reg < 3_reg AND PC' = 196;
25  PC = 196 AND 2_reg == 0 -> PC' = 242;
26  PC = 197 -> PC' = 198;
27  PC = 198 -> PC' = 200;
28  PC = 199 -> PC' = 200;
```

```
29 | PC = 200 -> lw(4_reg', memAdr(sp_reg, 48), _clk_) AND PC' = 201;
30 | PC = 201 -> 2_reg' = 0 +U 4 AND PC' = 202;
31 | PC = 202 -> 5_reg' = 0 +U 2_reg AND PC' = 203;
32 | PC = 203 -> sw(2_reg, memAdr(sp_reg, 32), _clk_) AND PC' = 204;
33 | PC = 204 -> ra_reg' = 206 AND PC' = 31;
34 | PC = 205 -> PC' = 206;
35 | PC = 206 -> 4_reg' = gp_reg +U getGlobalIndex(sensors) AND
36 |              PC' = 207;
37 | PC = 207 -> lw(5_reg', memAdr(sp_reg, 48), _clk_) AND PC' = 208;
38 | PC = 208 -> 2_reg' = 2_reg << 2 AND PC' = 209;
39 | PC = 209 -> lw(4_reg', memAdr(4_reg, 0), _clk_) AND PC' = 210;
40 | PC = 210 -> 3_reg' = 5_reg << 2 AND PC' = 211;
41 | PC = 211 -> 2_reg' = 4_reg +U 2_reg AND PC' = 212;
42 | PC = 212 -> 3_reg' = 4_reg +U 3_reg AND PC' = 213;
43 | PC = 213 -> lw(3_reg', memAdr(3_reg, 0), _clk_) AND PC' = 214;
44 | PC = 214 -> lw(2_reg', memAdr(2_reg, 0), _clk_) AND PC' = 215;
45 | PC = 215 -> sw(4_reg, memAdr(sp_reg, 28), _clk_) AND PC' = 216;
46 | PC = 216 -> 4_reg' = 0 +U 5_reg AND PC' = 217;
47 | PC = 217 -> lw(5_reg', memAdr(sp_reg, 32), _clk_) AND PC' = 218;
48 | PC = 218 -> sw(2_reg, memAdr(sp_reg, 24), _clk_) AND PC' = 219;
49 | PC = 219 -> sw(3_reg, memAdr(sp_reg, 20), _clk_) AND PC' = 220;
50 | PC = 220 -> ra_reg' = 222 AND PC' = 47;
51 | PC = 221 -> PC' = 222;
52 | PC = 222 -> 2_reg' = 2_reg << 2 AND PC' = 223;
53 | PC = 223 -> lw(3_reg', memAdr(sp_reg, 20), _clk_) AND PC' = 224;
54 | PC = 224 -> 3_reg' = 3_reg << 1 AND PC' = 225;
55 | PC = 225 -> 4_reg' = gp_reg +U getGlobalIndex(tmp) AND
56 |              PC' = 226;
57 | PC = 226 -> lw(5_reg', memAdr(sp_reg, 28), _clk_) AND PC' = 227;
58 | PC = 227 -> 2_reg' = 5_reg +U 2_reg AND PC' = 228;
59 | PC = 228 -> lw(6_reg', memAdr(sp_reg, 48), _clk_) AND PC' = 229;
60 | PC = 229 -> lw(2_reg', memAdr(2_reg, 0), _clk_) AND PC' = 230;
61 | PC = 230 -> lw(7_reg', memAdr(sp_reg, 24), _clk_) AND PC' = 231;
62 | PC = 231 -> 3_reg' = 7_reg -U 3_reg AND PC' = 232;
63 | PC = 232 -> lw(4_reg', memAdr(4_reg, 0), _clk_) AND PC' = 233;
```

```
64 | PC = 233 -> 6_reg' = 6_reg << 2 AND PC' = 234;
65 | PC = 234 -> 2_reg' = 3_reg +U 2_reg AND PC' = 235;
66 | PC = 235 -> 3_reg' = 4_reg +U 6_reg AND PC' = 236;
67 | PC = 236 -> sw(2_reg, memAdr(3_reg, 0), _clk_) AND PC' = 237;
68 | PC = 237 -> lw(2_reg', memAdr(sp_reg, 48), _clk_) AND PC' = 238;
69 | PC = 238 -> 2_reg' = 2_reg +U 1 AND PC' = 239;
70 | PC = 239 -> sw(2_reg, memAdr(sp_reg, 48), _clk_) AND PC' = 240;
71 | PC = 240 -> PC' = 193;
72 | PC = 241 -> PC' = 242;
73 | PC = 242 -> 2_reg' = gp_reg +U getGlobalIndex(worker1Ready) AND
74 |             PC' = 243;
75 | PC = 243 -> lw(4_reg', memAdr(2_reg, 0), _clk_) AND PC' = 244;
76 | PC = 244 -> ra_reg' = 246 AND PC' = 11;
77 | PC = 245 -> PC' = 246;
78 | PC = 246 -> lw(ra_reg', memAdr(sp_reg, 52), _clk_) AND
79 |             PC' = 247;
80 | PC = 247 -> sp_reg' = sp_reg +U 56 AND resetMem(sp_reg, 56) AND
81 |             PC' = 248;
82 | PC = 248 -> PC' = ra_reg;
83 | PC = 249 -> PC' = 250;
```

3.3 The MEMICS Task Model

For a proper support of task-based systems used in the automotive domain like AUTOSAR and OSEK the MEMICS Model has been extended. The resulting task model features a set of tasks $R = \{r_1, \ldots, r_p\}$. Each task r_j is defined over the subset of states $S' = \{s_{j_1}, \ldots, s_{j_k}\}$ and the subset of transitions $T' = \{t_{j'_1}, \ldots, t_{j'_l}\}$ of the original MEMICS Model M. The transition $t_{j'_i}$ of a task r_j is defined as the 4-tuple: $< s_{j_i}, a, c, s'_{j_i} >$, like in the original MEMICS Model. In addition a tasks requires the parameters:

core, prio, preempt, freq, idle, start, run, wait.

The parameter **core** specifies to which processor core the task is assigned, and **prio** defines the priority of the task, which is required for scheduling. The parameter **freq** defines the cycle-time (frequency) of a task in milliseconds, so e. g., a 10*ms* task has the frequency 10. The **preempt** parameter declares, whether the task is cooperative or preemptive and can therefore be interrupted during execution by any task with higher priority. The four remaining parameters **idle**, **start**, **run** and **wait** are required to model a proper scheduling among all tasks of a system modeled in MEMICS. The different scheduling states of one task are illustrated in Figure 3.4.

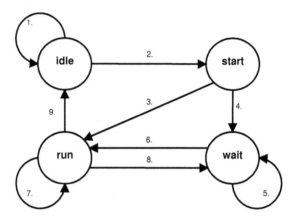

Figure 3.4. The Scheduler of a Task inside MEMICS represented by a State Machine

Let's assume a task is initially in the **idle** state – whereas at the start of a verification run, all tasks are either set to **run** or **wait** according to their priority. Depending on the frequency of a task, the system puts the task periodically and correspondingly into the **start** state. From here, the scheduler decides – depending on the priority of the task and on the current state of all other tasks on the same core –, whether the current task can be executed (**run**) or has to **wait**. Once a task finished its execution, it returns to the **idle** state. In order to provide a correct scheduling of all tasks t_j on one processor core and the assumption that the tasks on this core are ordered according to their priority from highest (1) to lowest (n), the following rules must hold:

Transition 1: **idle$_i$** $\wedge$ **clk%(freq$_i$)** $\neq$ **0** $\rightarrow$ **idle$_i$**

In case task i is currently in state **idle** and is not triggered according to its frequency, it remains in **idle**.

Transition 2: $\text{idle}_i \wedge \text{clk}\%(\text{freq}_i) = 0 \rightarrow \text{start}_i$
The scheduler starts the activation of task i, which is currently in **idle**, resulting in a switch into the **start** state.

Transition 3:
$$\text{start}_i \wedge \bigwedge_{f=1}^{i-1} \text{start}_f + \text{run}_f + \text{wait}_f = 0 \wedge \bigwedge_{k=i+1}^{n} \text{run}_k + !\text{preempt}_k \leqslant 1 \rightarrow \text{run}_i$$
If there exists no task t_f, which is currently either in state **start**, **run** or **wait**, with higher priority then t_i and in addition there is no task t_k, which is currently running and is cooperative, with a lower priority, the task t_i can be finally activated and is entering the state **run**.

Transition 4:
$$\text{start}_i \wedge \bigvee_{f=1}^{i-1} \text{start}_f + \text{run}_f + \text{wait}_f \neq 0 \wedge \bigvee_{k=i+1}^{n} \text{run}_k + !\text{preempt}_k = 2 \rightarrow \text{wait}_i$$
Otherwise, if there exists one task t_f with higher priority, which is currently in state **start**, **run** or **wait**, or if one task t_k with lower priority is running and cooperative, the task t_i must be waiting for at least one more cycle.

Transition 5:
$$\text{wait}_i \wedge \bigvee_{f=1}^{i-1} \text{start}_f + \text{run}_f + \text{wait}_f \neq 0 \vee \bigvee_{k=i+1}^{n} \text{run}_k + !\text{preempt}_k = 2 \rightarrow \text{wait}_i$$
In case task t_i is waiting and there exists one task t_f, which is currently in state **start**, **run** or **wait**, or there exists one task t_k, which is currently running and can not be interrupted, the task t_i must remain in the **wait** state.

Transition 6:
$$\text{wait}_i \wedge \bigvee_{f=1}^{i-1} \text{start}_f + \text{run}_f + \text{wait}_f = 0 \wedge \bigwedge_{k=i+1}^{n} \text{run}_k + !\text{preempt}_k \leqslant 1 \rightarrow \text{run}_i$$
If the task t_i is waiting and no task t_f is in state **start**, **run** or **wait** and no task t_k is running and can not be preempted, t_i is activated and switches to state **run**.

Transition 7: $\text{run}_i \wedge !\text{preempt}_i \vee \bigvee_{f=1}^{i-1} \text{start}_f + \text{wait}_f = 0 \rightarrow \text{run}_i$
Task t_i, which is currently running, remains in the **run** state, if it is either cooperative or no other task t_f with higher priority exists, which is currently in state **start** or **wait**.

Transition 8: $\mathbf{run_i} \wedge \mathbf{preempt_i} \wedge \bigvee\limits_{f=1}^{i-1} \mathbf{start_f} + \mathbf{wait_f} \neq 0 \rightarrow \mathbf{wait_i}$

In case the preemptive task t_i is running and there exists one other task t_f, which is currently in state **start** or **wait**, the task t_i must switch to **wait**.

Transition 9: $\mathbf{run_i} \wedge \mathbf{currentInst_i} = \mathbf{terminatorInst} \rightarrow \mathbf{idle_i}$

Once the last instruction of the running task t_i is passed, t_i switches to the **idle** state and waits for its next activation.

General Rule: $\sum\limits_{j=1}^{n} \mathbf{run_j} \leqslant 1$

This rule ensures that only one task t_j is actually running at one time, since only one atomic operation can be processed by one core.

In order to operate with respect to the synchronization instruction `waitOnEvent`, MEMICS reschedules the system during the period a task is waiting for an event. Under consideration of these rules, MEMICS is able to model an entire task based system like AUTOSAR or OSEK, although those systems provide common interrupt service routines (ISR), which can possibly interfere with any task at any time. In order to be safe from possible runtime errors, MEMICS constrains the author of sources to be analyzed with MEMICS, to secure all critical sections – e. g., access to global memory – by at least disabling all ISRs. On the other hand this ensures more safety of the source code and in addition reduces the search space of MEMICS considerably.

3.3.1 MEMICS Virtual System Configuration

This section shows the configuration of the virtual system modeling the ECU in MEMICS. This includes the hardware with the CPU and memory, as well as the operating system, including tasks, interrupt service routines, synchronization and so on. The format of the configuration has been derived from the general OIL standard. For details refer to Section 2.1.1. The configuration is divided into the different sections: **the basis system, tasks, Interrupt Service Routines (ISRs)**, and **alarms, counters and events**.

Listing 3.2 shows the configuration for the system, an ISR and a task. The system configures the CPU with a number of cores and the frequency in MHz with which it is running. In addition the available amount of system RAM has to be defined in MB. Although the type of memory alignment is configurable, the alignment is specified per default to 4 byte.

Listing 3.2. MEMICS System Configuration: The System, ISR and Task

```
1   SYSTEM {                          |     MAXCYCLE   = <int>;
2     NUMOFCORES   = <int>;           |   };
3     FREQUENCY    = <int> MHz;       |
4     MEMSIZE      = <int> MB;        |   TASK {
5   ---------------------------       |     NAME         = <string>;
6     MEMALIGN     = <int> bytes;     |     FREQUENCY    = <int> ms;
7   };                                |     PRIORITY     = <int>;
8                                     |     CORE         = <int>;
9   ISR {                             |     PREEMPTIVE   = <bool>;
10    NAME        = <string>;         |   ---------------------------
11    CATEGORY    = <bool>;           |     STACKSIZE    = <int>;
12  ---------------------------       |     EVENT        = <string>;
13    RESOURCE    = <string>;         |     RESOURCE     = <string>;
14    MINCYCLE    = <int>;            |   };
```

A task is defined by a unique id, its name, which in MEMICS has to be exactly the name of the entry function of the task. In addition its frequency in ms, the priority – required by the scheduler – and the core it is assigned to, have to be specified. The configuration also includes a flag, whether the task is preemptive or not. The stacksize is an obligatory configuration item, its default value set to 1024 byte. In case a task requires synchronization via an event, the corresponding event(s) has(have) to be specified here. Also the resource is an obligatory configuration item. In terms of OSEK a resource describes a behavior like e. g., a mutex or a semaphore. The name of an ISR is again its unique identifier and in addition the corresponding function entry point. The Boolean category flag determines, if the interrupt is hardware- or software-based. The definition of the resource is similar to the one for a task. The two configuration items MINCYCLE and MAXCYCLE can be used to help MEMICS reduce the search space with respect to the ISR, by defining the observed time intervals in which an ISR must occur once.

3. The MEMICS Software Verification Approach

Listing 3.3 presents the configuration for alarms, counters and events. A counter is defined by a unique name and has a fixed number of enumerations defined as NUMCYCLES. An event is simply defined by a unique identifier name. Unlike in OSEK, where the specification of an event has to be unique corresponding to a waiting task, is the relation between tasks and events surjective in MEMICS. This is required, in order to activate more than one task on different cores simultaneously. An event is triggered by the SETEVENT routine, shown in the configuration of ALARM1. An alarm is defined by its name as a unique identifier and must in addition have a counter object. The second alarm (ALARM2) is used to directly activate tasks.

Listing 3.3. MEMICS System Configuration: Alarm, Counter and Event

```
 1   COUNTER {                        |    EVENT {
 2     NAME        = <string>;        |      NAME = <string>;
 3     NUMCYCLES   = <int>;           |    };
 4   };                               |
 5                                    |
 6   ALARM1 {                         |    ALARM2 {
 7     NAME    = <string>;            |      NAME     = <string>;
 8     COUNTER = <string>;            |      COUNTER  = <string>;
 9     ACTION  = SETEVENT {           |      ACTION   = ACTIVATETASK {
10       EVENT = <string>;            |        TASK   = <string>;
11     };                             |      };
12   };                               |    };
```

3.3.1 Example (The MEMICS Model Configuration for the Automotive Race Condition Example).

The system configuration for the running Example 2.3.1 is shown in Listing 3.4. The hardware of this system consists of a CPU with three cores, running at 50MHz, and features 256MB of RAM, which is 4-byte aligned. The corresponding software contains the two 10ms tasks readInputs and writeOutputs, which are both running on the first core and are in cooperative mode – non-preemptive. The two tasks computing the Laplace operator worker1 and worker2 are also scheduled in the 10ms slot and are both also non-preemptive. But worker1 is

assigned to the second core and worker2 to the third. In addition the configuration contains the four events data1Ready, data2Ready, worker1Ready, and
worker2Ready, which are required for communication among the tasks.

Listing 3.4. MEMICS Virtual System Configuration for the Automotive Race Condition
Example

```
 1  SYSTEM {                    |   TASK {
 2    NUMOFCORES = 3;           |     NAME = worker1;
 3    FREQUENCY = 50;           |     FREQUENCY = 10;
 4    MEMSIZE = 256;            |     PRIORITY = 1;
 5    MEMALIGN = 4;             |     CORE = 1;
 6  };                          |     PREEMPTIVE = 0;
 7                              |     EVENT = data1Ready;
 8  TASK {                      |   };
 9    NAME = readInputs;        |
10    FREQUENCY = 10;           |   TASK {
11    PRIORITY = 1;             |     NAME = worker2;
12    CORE = 0;                 |     FREQUENCY = 10;
13    PREEMPTIVE = 0;           |     PRIORITY = 1;
14  };                          |     CORE = 2;
15                              |     PREEMPTIVE = 0;
16  TASK {                      |     EVENT = data2Ready;
17    NAME = writeOutputs;      |   };
18    FREQUENCY = 10;           |
19    PRIORITY = 2;             |   EVENT {
20    CORE = 0;                 |     NAME = data1Ready;
21    PREEMPTIVE = 0;           |   };
22    EVENT = worker1Ready;     |   EVENT {
23    EVENT = worker2Ready;     |     NAME = data2Ready;
24  };                          |   };
25                              |
26  EVENT {                     |   EVENT {
27    NAME = worker1Ready;      |     NAME = worker2Ready;
28  };                          |   };
```

3.4   The MEMICS Core

In the MEMICS Core the actual verification is performed by a Bounded Model Checking (BMC) approach of the MEMICS Model. Note that, compared to common BMC, the property to check is in most of the cases not encoded into the formula, but encoded into the proof engine. However, it is still possible to pass a property to MEMICS as input, like e. g., a label in the source code to be reached. An overview of this process is shown in Figure 3.5.

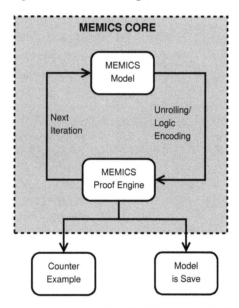

Figure 3.5. Overview of the Core of the MEMICS Software Verification Approach

The MEMICS Model is unwound step by step into a logic formula, which is passed to the internal proof engine. This proof engine checks, if the current formula contains any kind of runtime error or not. If an error is found the engine can return the specific trace leading to it. In the other case, the process continues with a new unrolling step. The process is running until a runtime error is identified, the source code is proven to be safe – in respect to the errors

MEMICS is able to detect –, or a timeout occurred.

3.4.1 Unrolling of the MEMICS Model

The efficiency of model unrolling has a large impact on the runtime complexity in BMC. Most common tools provide a simple unrolling mechanism, which unrolls the entire model at each iteration and encodes it in SSA form. The resulting formula of such an unrolling is of size $O(nk)$, with the assumption that the model consists of n possible transitions among the states and the current iteration is k. MEMICS unrolls only the current set of relevant instructions, which results in a fewer number of clauses. This unrolling process is illustrated in Example 3.4.1.

3.4.1 Example (Model Unrolling).
Assume the relevant program control flow is the one shown in Figure 3.6. The transition from state s_1 to s_2 is unrolled straight forward. The state s_2 represents a basic C if-statement, which branches depending on the truth value of the condition c_1. In case this truth value is unique, MEMICS strictly unrolls either the true branch towards the state s_3 or the false branch s_4, only. Otherwise both transitions have to be unrolled, which results in a set of two successor states s_3 and s_4. Respectively to the set of successor states, the unrolling continues until the join state s_{i-1} has been reached, regardless of whether the if-branch, the else-branch or both branches have been unwound. The transition to state s_i is again straight forward. The construct around the state s_i is a simple loop, which runs depending on the truth value of the condition c_2, defined by the sequence $(s_i \rightarrow s_{i+1} \rightarrow \ldots \rightarrow s_{m-1} \rightarrow s_{i-1})$. In case the loop condition is true the sequence is unrolled or if it is false the transition towards state s_m is unrolled, only. If the condition results in an unknown truth value, both cases have to be unrolled. The unrolling process is finished, if the only remaining state in the set to unroll is s_{end}.

The current implementation of MEMICS features three different modes of model unrolling: **basic, task-based** and **path-based**.

basic: The **basic** unrolling mode is defined for common C/C++ programs. In this case the model is unwound exactly as described in Example 3.4.1.

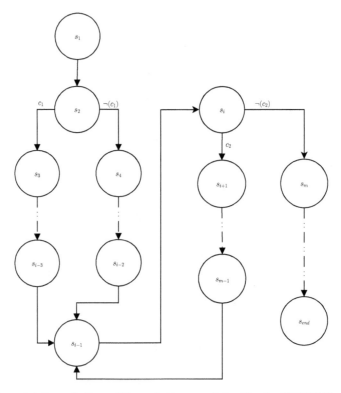

Figure 3.6. Example Control Flow of a Program defined by the MEMICS Model

task-based: The **task-based** unrolling mode, is an extended basic unrolling, which includes all the relevant scheduling rules for all tasks – as defined in Section 3.3. In addition, if the unrolling process is able to decide if one task is not active at all, the according task is not unrolled until it becomes active, again.

path-based: In **path-based** unrolling mode MEMICS creates entire paths leading to a specific target, only. The search for such a target is currently implemented breadth first in MEMICS.

3.4.2 The MEMICS Interval Constraint Solver

The backend of MEMICS is an Interval Constraint Solver (ICS), which is specialized with respect to program analysis, where the focus on the MIPS assembly language including its memory operations. The ICS in general is based on the ideas from HySAT and its successor iSAT. The main solve routine of MEMICS, which is illustrated in pseudo-code in Listing 3.5, is an implementation of the BMC approach.

Listing 3.5. The MEMICS Overall BMC Algorithm

```
1  bool solve() {
2    result = false;
3    while (!foundRuntimeError && !EOF) {
4      // unroll the next set of instructions
5      if (update())
6        // start the actual search
7        result = search();
8    }
9    return result;
10 }
```

The process is running as long as no runtime error can be found or if otherwise it has traversed the entire sources (EOF). In the first step, the solver updates its clause database by calling the unroll-routine of the underlying model. In case the unrolling of the current iteration raises a trivial conflict, the solver straight drops towards the next iteration. In order to check for such a trivial conflict, the update-routine contains a preprocessing unit. This preprocessing unit fires the first initial unit propagation steps on the current clause database. If there exists any clause, which is in conflict with the current variable assignments, the entire formula cannot be fulfilled – at least in this iteration. In case the update process succeeded, the solver starts the actual search process, which is the core routine of any SAT-/SMT-Solver.

The main search procedure of MEMICS is based on the Davis Putnam Loveland Logemann (DPLL) algorithm, like HySAT and iSAT. In Listing 3.6 a pseudocode like implementation of the search algorithm is shown.

Listing 3.6. The MEMICS Search Algorithm based on DPLL

```
1   bool search() {
2     // run until a runtime error is found
3     while (!foundRuntimeError) {
4       // propagate all current decisions,
5       // and check for any conflict
6       conflict = icp();
7       // in case a conflict is raised, check if its
8       // reasonable and try to remove it from the tree
9       if (conflict) {
10        // conflicts on decision level 0 are invalid
11        if (DL == 0) return false;
12        newDL = analyze(conflict, &learnt);
13        backtrackAndAddClause(newDL, learnt);
14      }
15      // otherwise a new variable decision takes place
16      else {
17        // no more variables available
18        if (varQueue.empty()) {
19          // target mode -> error location reached
20          if (searchForTarget) return true;
21          // check for alternate paths
22          if (!checkForPaths(&other, &newDL)
23            return false;
24          else
25            backtrackAndAddClause(newDL, other);
26        }
27        // decide the next variable
28        else
29          decide();
30      }
31    }
32  }
```

The search algorithm runs until either: a runtime error has been found (line:

3), a unresolvable conflict occurs (line: 11), a specific target has been reached (line: 20), or all possible program paths have been traversed (line: 23). In the first step the algorithm runs the Interval Constraint Propagation (ICP), which, in case there exists a conflict according to the current assignment, returns the conflicting clause. If a conflict occurred during ICP, the solver analyzes the current trail and computes the cause of the conflict. In case such a cause is identifiable, a learnt clause is generated, which eliminates the exact trail from all succeeding runs. Therefore, the solver backtracks the trail towards to corresponding backtrack level and adds the learnt clause to its clause database. If on the other hand ICP did not raise any conflict, the solver switches into the decision state. In the decision state, the solver checks whether the variable queue is empty or not. If the queue is empty, all currently available variables have a pending assignment and the solver either returns – in case a specific target has been defined – or checks for other paths, which either results in backtracking towards that new path and the search continues or the search terminates – indicating that the current iteration is free of any runtime error.

In the following several subroutines of the search process are introduced in detail: icp in Subsection 3.4.2.1, analyze in Subsection 3.4.2.2 and decide in Subsection 3.4.2.4.

3.4.2.1 Interval Constraint Propagation (ICP)

The propagation step – in case of MEMICS: Interval Constraint Propagation – is the heart of all state of the art solvers based on the DPLL algorithm. In the propagation step the solver tries to fulfill a literal of a clause, which is unit under the current assignment and therefore must be true in order to fulfill the entire clause. If the procedure is not able to fulfill the current literal, the clause it belongs to is in conflict with the current assignment and is therefore returned as conflict clause. In [42] HySAT/iSAT was used as a backend-end solver, but once the source files to analyze outreached a few hundred lines of code, the approach did not scale any more. As aforementioned, the main reasons therefore are located in the unrolling procedure, and the lack of assembly language specific theories in the solver, which require a lot of additional definitions in the logic formula. In order to properly verify software and overcome the observed problems, the ICP procedure of MEMICS has been equipped with a lot of new features. Therefore the main ICP routine has been split up into several parts, like the basic arithmetic, memory access routines and type specific routines. Each of these icp routines is introduced in detail in the following.

icpArithmetic

The icpArithmetic routine covers all kind of arithmetic interval propagations. During this deduction process, each operation is checked for any kind of runtime error like e. g., an arithmetic over-/underflow or a division by zero. In addition, MEMICS features, compared to iSAT, also bitwise operations on integer values, like e. g., arithmetic and, or and shift operations. All these operations are also handled in the icpArithmetic routine.

icpFree

In the icpFree operation a common free or delete instruction is propagated. The operation checks if the address to be freed itself is valid, including the amount of bytes to be freed. Two cases have to be distinguished: a propagation at decision level (DL) zero or any other DL. On DL zero the memory is just freed. Otherwise the free operation has to be tracked in the free table and in addition the current memory entries have to be backed up on top because the operation can possibly get reverted during the search process, when the solver triggers the backtracking mechanism.

icpLoad

icpLoad represents the load operation of MEMICS. It can load a byte, a half-word, a word and a long-word from the internal memory. The solver checks, if the underlying memory area is allocated and throws a null dereference, if not. In addition it checks for uninitialized memory and warns the user, if one is found. All the load operations are tracked, together with the store operations, in a memory access table in order to identify race conditions with MEMICS. In Section 3.4.6 these race checks are described in detail.

icpMalloc

icpMalloc is used to allocate memory. Therefore, an allocation table tracks all allocations and is used to determine the next free memory address for a malloc request. In case the virtual MEMICS Model runs out of memory an exception is thrown.

icpMemcpy/icpMemset

icpMemcpy and icpMemset are used to handle memcpy- and memset-like operations internally. The memcpy operation requires the destination address, the source address and the amount of bytes to be copied. The memset operation requires the destination address, the value and the amount of bytes to be set. The solver checks on both operations if the memory behind the address is allocated and respectively throws a null dereference. Additionally it checks the memcpy operation for uninitialized memory at the source memory and warns the user.

icpStore

icpStore represents the store operation. Like the load operation it supports byte-, half-word-, word- and long-word-wise access to the memory. The operation is also checked for null dereferences. Additionally also each store operation is tracked in a memory access table, in order to identify race conditions, which is described in Section 3.4.6.

3.4.2.2 Conflict Analysis and Backtracking

The conflict analysis in MEMICS works in general like any common state of the art SAT conflict analysis. The analysis algorithm in short is shown in Listing 3.7. Generally the algorithm searches for all pending decisions towards the actual conflict, until the first unit implication points (UIP). If no such a first UIP is found the algorithm creates a new literal consisting out of the negated bound of the current pending decision and adds it to the learnt clause. Otherwise the algorithm gathers all decisions on the current path until all first UIPs are identified and the entire learnt clause is generated. This learnt clause ensures that the exact conflict can not occur any more in all succeeding runs of the search process. At the end of the algorithm the learnt clause is checked for possible duplicate literals, which are then erased from it. And finally the backtrack level for the current learnt clause is computed and returned.

Listing 3.7. The Analyze Algorithm to Calculate the Reasons for a Conflict

```
1   int analyze(clause* conflict, clause* learnt) {
2     int backtrackDL = -1;
3     decisionVec decs = conflict->getReasons();
4
5     while (!decs.empty()) {
6       decisionVec newDecs;
7       for (iterator d in decs) {
8         // In case decision d has reasons, add them to
9         // the queue
10        if (!d.getReasons().empty())
11          newDecs.insert(d.getReasons());
12        // if the decision is just based on a variable
13        // decision, add the negated relation to learnt
14        // clause
15        else if (d.getData() == NULL) {
16            Lit l(d.getVar(), not(d.getRel()), d.getOp());
17            learnt.addLit(l);
18        }
19      }
20      decs.clear();
21      decs.insert(newDecs);
22    }
23
24    learnt = eraseDuplicates(learnt);
25    backtrackDL = findBacktrackDL(learnt);
26
27    return backtrackDL;
28  }
```

3.4.2.3 Variable Queue

The variable queue is one of the heart pieces in a state of the art SAT-/SMT-Solver. Usually this queue contains all those variables, which are not initially assigned with a fix point value via unit propagation. Since the focus of MEMICS is program analysis, where the program defines a specific control flow, the variable queue is sorted corresponding to this control flow. Otherwise the solver might be able to find a satisfying assignment according to common SAT-/SMT-Rules, but this assignment would be a false positive with respect to the program. Therefore, the variables in the queue are ordered based on their "temporal" occurrence in the control flow. And, in addition, the queue only contains the registers of all instructions, and no state flow information like program counter variables. The reason therefore resides in the fact that with the decision of the next variable from the queue, one of the occurrences of the corresponding program counter variable becomes unit.

3.4.2.4 Decision Step

In the decision step the solver pulls the next variable from the variable queue, splits up its current interval and assigns it with the new result. In general two different cases have to be considered: the variable is of Boolean type or not. Since the interval of a Boolean variable is defined as $[0, 1]$, the result of the interval split is always a point. In the current implementation of MEMICS all Boolean variables are assigned to zero in the decision step. For all other variable types, also two different cases have to be considered: if the variable is contained in a relational clause or not. In case the variable x – with the current interval $[a, b]$ – is not contained in a conditional clause, its interval is split to $[(b - a)/2, b]$, per default. If the variable is on the other hand contained in a conditional clause, the solver differs between the following two clause types:

$$\textbf{I. } (x \ \text{rel}_{op} \ y) \ \text{or} \ \textbf{II. } x := (y \ \text{rel}_{op} \ z).$$

I. Assume the variable to decide is x. This deduces a new interval for x such that the truth-value of the relation rel_{op} is fulfilled. This might possibly also result in a new interval for the variable y.

II. The solver has to consider two different variants: a) the variable to decide is on the left-hand side, or b) the variable is on the right-hand side.

a) In this case the variable x can be treated as a simple Boolean variable. Hence, no matter what truth-value the solver assigns to x, the following has to hold:

$$(x) \Leftrightarrow (y \; \mathrm{rel_{op}} \; z)$$

In addition this implies the resulting new intervals for y and z in order to match the truth-value of the left-hand side.

b) In this case the variable itself has to be treated like in case **I.**. In addition also the resulting value for the Boolean variable x has to be retrieved.

3.4.3 Arithmetic Runtime Errors

As illustrated in Table 2.3, MEMICS currently detects the arithmetic runtime errors: division by zero, overflow and underflow. Therefore, the solver checks at each division, if the interval of the dividend contains the zero, and raises respectively an error. For the detection of an over- or underflow, the solver logs each arithmetic operation of type signed integer, if an upper or respectively lower wrap around occurs.

3.4.4 Memory Runtime Errors

The detection of a double free error is also handled by the malloc and free tables, which have been introduced in Subsection 3.4.2.1. A tracking entry of the free table can only be deleted from the table, if the solver backtracks past the free operation. In case the solver detects that the memory region to be freed is currently not allocated and has already been freed, a double free error is thrown.

For the detection of an invalid free error, the solver uses the internal malloc table. In case the base address to be freed is not trackable in the malloc table and is not covered by a double free error, the solver throws an invalid free error.

Each memory address located inside the virtual memory of MEMICS, contains a flag, which states whether the memory behind the address is currently null or not. This flag is used by the solver to identify null dereference errors.

The error class sizeof on pointers covers a very nasty programming error. A sizeof operation on a pointer only returns the size of the pointer itself, which in case of a 32-bit machine is 4 bytes. Though, e. g., the structure behind the pointer contains an int32, a double and an int8, the actual size of this structure is 13 byte or depending on the internal alignment, e. g., 16 byte. Hence, the actual error is usually a corrupt memory problem, since the access of an element in the structure, exceeds the allocated memory region.

The use after free error detection is using the free table in combination with the null flag of a memory address. In case the current propagation step acquires access to a memory region, which is currently null and in addition has been freed, the solver throws a use after free error.

3.4.5 Pointer Arithmetic Errors

The runtime error invalid range covers e. g., the basic error index out of bounds. Since MEMICS is operating directly on assembly code, it is not possible to identify exactly an index out of bounds error, because the actual access of the error is a basic null dereference. Though it correctly detects all of them.

Also the detection of the runtime error class pointer scaling, is covered by the memory null flag. A common error for this class is e. g.:

$$\text{int *p = (int*)malloc(sizeof(int)); int8 *p2 = (int8*)(p+1); *p2 = 1;}$$

In this example, the programmer allocates an int pointer (p) and wants to assign the second byte inside p to an int8 pointer. However, the cast statement assigns p2 with the address pointing to the first byte behind the memory region of p. This can lead to a null dereference.

3.4.6 Concurrent Runtime Errors

In order to detect locking errors, the user must define for the solver, which function is representing the locking mechanism. With this information the solver is able to detect a dead lock scenario among two and more different tasks. Whenever a task acquires a lock of a resource, the solver logs the task and the locked resource in an internal table. This log entry is deleted once the corresponding unlock routine is called. For the identification of a dead lock the following rule must hold:

$$\exists \text{task}_i, \text{task}_j :$$
$$\text{lock}(\text{res}_k, \text{task}_i) \wedge \text{lock}(\text{res}_l, \text{task}_j) \wedge \text{req\_lock}(\text{res}_l, \text{task}_i) \wedge \text{req\_lock}(\text{res}_k, \text{task}_j)$$

3. The MEMICS Software Verification Approach

This rule is extendable to a variable number of tasks and an arbitrary complexity among the interleavings of locked resources. For the detection of a double lock error, the following rule must hold:

$$\exists task_i : lock(res_k, task_i) \wedge req\_lock(res_k, task_i)$$

The error detection of a race condition including a lost update (non-repeatable-read) is achieved via a table, in which all accesses to the internal memory are logged. An entry in this table is defined as:

```
(<memory address> ; <access type> ; <task> ; <clk_cycle>)
```

Using this table, MEMICS is then able to identify the concurrent error classes: non-repeatable-read, read-after-write and write-after-write. In order to identify such an error, the corresponding rule from Table 3.12 must hold.

Table 3.12. Rules for the Detection of Concurrent Runtime Errors

Error:	Rule:
non-repeatable-read	$(adr_r; r; task_i; clk_k) \wedge (adr_r; r; task_i; clk_l) \wedge$ $(adr_t; w; task_j; clk_m) \wedge adr_r = adr_s = adr_t \wedge$ $clk_l - clk_k \leqslant cycle\_time(task_i) \wedge$ $clk_k < clk_m \leqslant clk_l$
read-after-write	$(adr_r; r; task_i; clk_k) \wedge (adr_s; w; task_j; clk_l) \wedge$ $adr_r = adr_s \wedge clk_l - clk_k \leqslant cycle\_time(task_i) \wedge$ $clk_k < clk_l$
write-after-write	$(adr_r; w; task_i; clk_k) \wedge (adr_s; w; task_j; clk_l) \wedge$ $adr_r = adr_s \wedge clk_l - clk_k \leqslant cycle\_time(task_i) \wedge$ $clk_k < clk_l$

The cycle_time defines one execution cycle of a task, including its wait-cycles in case it is preemptive. According to the rules a non-repeatable-read error is detected, if one task ($task_i$) is reading a resource (adr_r) at two different times (clk_k and clk_l) within one cycle and a second task ($task_j$) is writing to the same resource in between these two reads. A read-after-write error is raised, whenever there exists a task ($task_i$), which is reading a resource (adr_r) at time (clk_k), and there exists another task ($task_j$), which has written to the same resource in the current execution cycle of $task_i$ before the time-point clk_k. The solver identifies a write-after-write error, if there exist the two tasks ($task_i$ and $task_j$), which are both writing to the same resource and the time-point of these two accesses occurs in the intersection of both execution cycles.

The error detection of type missing synchronization, also requires the definition of the used synchronization functionality. With this information, the solver checks at each access to global memory, whether before and after the access, the corresponding synchronization methods are called.

3.4.7 Analysis Modes

The MEMICS software verification approach features two different operating modes:

▷ On the fly Analysis, and

▷ Target driven Analysis.

These two modes are introduced in the following.

3.4.7.1 On the fly Analysis

The operation mode: "On the fly Analysis" is the default mode of MEMICS. In this mode, MEMICS starts the search for any type of runtime error at the entry point the user has specified (per default, the main function). Unless MEMICS finds any error, it traverses over all possible branches reachable from the given root. In case of concurrent code, this includes also all permutations of possible interleavings among tasks. Note that the number of possible interleavings is limited by the priority of the tasks, as defined in Section 3.3. If MEMICS identifies any type of error, it immediately stops and notifies the user of the finding. In case the user asked for the detailed path, MEMICS provides it in addition to the error description and location.

3.4.7.2 Target driven Analysis

In Target driven Analysis mode, the user has to specify a certain target or property MEMICS has to check. Compared to the default mode, MEMICS only searches those branches, on which the target is reachable from the root node. The user can in addition configure, whether he or she wants MEMICS to stop and report errors, it finds on those paths, before reaching the actual target. In case the user disables this option, it can be possible that MEMICS reports a target reachable, which is only possible due to an error in the code before.

Chapter 4

Tests and Results

MEMICS has been tested on a various number of benchmarks, in order to check its correctness against several types of runtime errors. One benchmark suite at Daimler is based on runtime errors met in an industrial context, which is used to evaluate static software analysis tools. In the first tests, MEMICS had to successfully verify all those benchmarks covering the runtime errors from Table 2.3. MEMICS passed this test successfully. The results of MEMICS competing against several state of the art tools from the software verification competition [89] in 2013 (SV-Comp13) are shown in Section 4.1. Section 4.2 introduces the results of MEMICS for the running automotive Example 2.3.1.

4.1 Comparison against State of the Art Tools

In this section MEMICS has to compete against several state of the art tools on categories from the SV-Comp13. All the problems used in this competition are constructed as reachability problems – except for the category memory safety. For this purpose the label "ERROR" has been introduced, which has to be reached in case of an unsafe test case. Otherwise the tool has to prove the non-reachability of this label. Since, MEMICS and almost any of the competing tools are working based on a BMC approach the reachability analysis over infinite loops has to be treated with care. Real safety in terms of non-reachability of an error region can not be guaranteed by pure BMC. Such an approach can only ensure safety up to a fixed depth.

All results presented in this section have been obtained from runs on a machine with the Intel(R) Core(TM) i7-3517U CPU running at 1.9GHz and 10GB of RAM. The operating system is Ubuntu [90] version 13.10. Therefore, all the competitive tools have been downloaded from the competition web page. This guaranties a fair competition among the tools. Please note, the results obtained during these tests differ from the results published on the website of the SV-Comp13 for some benchmarks.

Feature Checks   The feature checks category covers all kind of checks for common runtime errors in C source code – from basic assertions, memory allocation and so on towards nested switch statements. Figure 4.1 shows the runtime results and Figure 4.2 the memory consumption of the tools.

Note that the y-axis is in logarithmic scale. The runtime chart shows that MEMICS competes well against the other tools and is among the fastest. Though, in three test cases it needed a lot more time to solve the benchmark. These three benchmarks (stateful*) implement a loop over an undetermined iterator. The loop-body contains a switch statement, with four cases. The ERROR label is only reachable over the path, visiting each of these cases in a certain order. Since the current path iteration algorithm inside MEMICS is working based on breadth first search, MEMICS spends a lot of time on finding the correct path to the ERROR label.

Regarding the memory consumption of MEMICS the same results can be observed from the image. Except those three benchmarks, the memory consumption of the current implementation of MEMICS is in the average field of its competitors.

Though, MEMICS is not the fastest according to the runtime performance, it is the only tool able to successfully solve all the benchmarks in this category. With regard to soundness, MEMICS wins this category. This overall result is shown in Table 4.1.

Table 4.1. Overall Results of the Category Feature Checks from the Software Verification Competition 2013

	blast	esbmc	llbmc	memics	predator
Score (%):	84.0	83.0	98.0	100.0	87.0
Time (s):	471.02	41.83	7.94	101.23	13.44

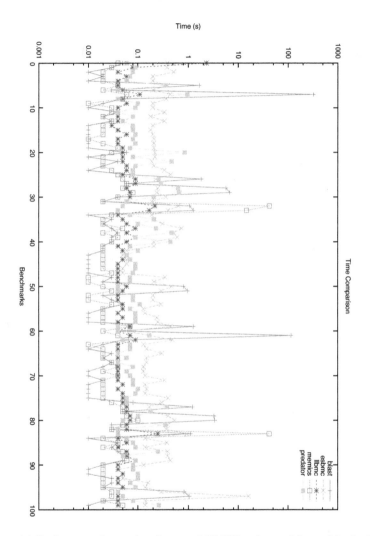

Figure 4.1. Performance Comparison between MEMICS and several State of the Art Tools for the Category Feature Checks: Runtime

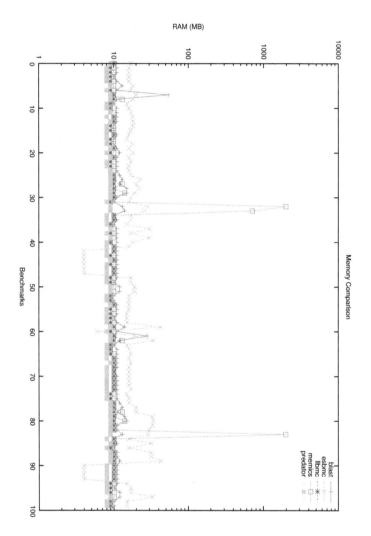

Figure 4.2. Performance Comparison between MEMICS and several State of the Art Tools for the Category Feature Checks: Memory Consumption

4.1. Comparison against State of the Art Tools

The detailed results of this category are shown in Table 4.2. The first block covers the pure C source files, whereas the second block contains source files, based on the same benchmarks, but these files are already preprocessed by a compiler. This preprocessing leads to additional information in the input source files, which may be responsible in the differences of the results for one benchmark by the same tool.

Table 4.2. Detailed Results of the Category Feature Checks from the Software Verification Competition 2013

Benchmark	blast		esbmc		libmc		memics		predator	
	Result	Time	Result	Time	Result	Time	Result	Time	Result	Time
1_3.c_unsafe.cil.c	unsafe	0.05	unsafe	0.39	unsafe	2.3	unsafe	0.04	unsafe	0.06
alias_of_return_2.c_safe_1.cil.c	safe	0.03	safe	0.38	safe	0.08	safe	0.03	safe	0.09
alias_of_return_2.c_safe.cil.c	safe	0.01	safe	0.52	safe	0.04	safe	0.02	safe	0.08
alias_of_return.c_safe_1.cil.c	safe	0.02	safe	0.2	safe	0.06	safe	0.02	safe	0.07
alias_of_return.c_safe.cil.c	safe	0.01	safe	0.2	safe	0.04	safe	0.02	safe	0.06
alt_test.c_unsafe.cil.c	unsafe	1.65	unsafe	0.39	unsafe	0.04	unsafe	0.04	unknown	0.36
callfpointer.c_unsafe.cil.c	unsafe	0.03	unsafe	0.2	unsafe	0.05	unsafe	0.02	unsafe	0.04
ex3_forlist.c_safe.cil.c	error	322.74	safe	0.44	safe	0.11	safe	0.06	safe	0.96
fo_test.c_unsafe.cil.c	unsafe	0.05	unsafe	0.37	unsafe	0.05	unsafe	0.05	unsafe	0.04
just_assert.c_safe.cil.c	safe	0.02	safe	0.2	safe	0.06	safe	0.01	safe	0.1
mutex_lock_int.c_safe_1.cil.c	safe	0.01	safe	0.2	safe	0.04	safe	0.03	safe	0.09
mutex_lock_int.c_unsafe.cil.c	unsafe	0.04	unsafe	0.34	unsafe	0.04	unsafe	0.03	unsafe	0.04
mutex_lock_struct.c_safe_1.cil.c	safe	0.02	safe	0.18	safe	0.04	safe	0.02	safe	0.08
mutex_lock_struct.c_unsafe.cil.c	unsafe	0.03	unsafe	0.34	unsafe	0.04	unsafe	0.03	unsafe	0.05
nested_structure.c_safe.cil.c	safe	0.01	safe	0.2	safe	0.03	safe	0.02	safe	0.08
nested_structure_noptr.c_safe.cil.c	safe	0.01	safe	0.18	safe	0.04	safe	0.02	safe	0.08
nested_structure_noptr_safe.c	safe	0.01	safe	0.2	safe	0.06	safe	0.02	safe	0.09
nested_structure_noptr_safe.cil.c	safe	0.01	safe	0.21	safe	0.04	safe	0.01	safe	0.08
nested_structure_ptr.c_safe.cil.c	safe	0.01	safe	0.21	safe	0.04	safe	0.02	safe	0.09
nested_structure_ptr_safe.c	safe	0.01	safe	0.21	safe	0.05	safe	0.04	safe	0.07
nested_structure_ptr_safe.cil.c	unsafe	0.06	unsafe	0.22	safe	0.05	safe	0.03	unknown	0.85
nested_structure_safe.c	safe	0.01	safe	0.22	safe	0.05	safe	0.02	safe	0.08
nested_structure_safe.cil.c	unsafe	0.04	unsafe	0.19	safe	0.05	safe	0.02	unknown	0.47
oomint.c_safe_1.cil.c	safe	0.02	safe	0.21	safe	0.06	safe	0.02	safe	0.09
oomint.c_safe.cil.c	safe	0.01	safe	0.34	safe	0.06	safe	0.03	safe	0.08
recursive_list.c_unsafe.cil.c	unsafe	0.07	unsafe	0.45	unsafe	0.05	unsafe	0.04	unknown	0.08
rule57_ebda_blast.c_safe_1.cil.c	safe	1.81	safe	0.23	safe	0.09	safe	0.05	unknown	0.26
rule57_ebda_blast.c_unsafe.cil.c	unsafe	0.06	unsafe	0.3	unsafe	0.09	unsafe	0.06	unknown	0.29
rule60_list2.c_safe.cil.c	safe	5.71	safe	0.25	safe	0.06	safe	0.05	safe	0.63
rule60_list2.c_unsafe_1.cil.c	unsafe	6.73	unsafe	0.24	unsafe	0.07	unsafe	0.08	unsafe	0.66
rule60_list.c_safe.cil.c	safe	0.04	unsafe	0.36	safe	0.07	safe	0.04	unknown	0.21
sizeofparameters_test.c_safe.cil.c	safe	0.02	safe	0.19	safe	0.06	safe	0.02	safe	0.06
stateful_check_unsafe.c	unsafe	1.07	unsafe	0.64	unsafe	0.22	unsafe	41.99	unsafe	0.05
stateful_check_unsafe.cil.c	unsafe	1.25	unsafe	0.4	unsafe	0.17	unsafe	14.65	unsafe	0.04
structure_assignment.c_safe.cil.c	safe	0.01	safe	0.19	safe	0.04	safe	0.03	safe	0.07
test_address.c_safe.cil.c	unsafe	0.03	safe	0.21	safe	0.05	safe	0.02	unknown	0.21
test_cut_trace.c_safe.cil.c	safe	0.02	safe	0.31	safe	0.06	safe	0.02	safe	0.1
test_malloc-1_safe.c	unsafe	0.03	safe	0.74	error	0.09	safe	0.05	safe	0.23
test_malloc-1_safe.cil.c	unsafe	0.04	safe	0.52	safe	0.06	safe	0.02	unknown	0.47
test_malloc-2_safe.c	unsafe	0.03	safe	0.61	error	0.09	safe	0.04	safe	0.09
test_malloc-2_safe.cil.c	unsafe	0.03	safe	0.21	safe	0.06	safe	0.03	unknown	0.45
test_overflow.c_safe.cil.c	safe	0.02	safe	0.21	safe	0.04	safe	0.02	safe	0.07
test_union_cast-1_safe.c	safe	0.02	error	0.06	safe	0.05	safe	0.02	safe	0.1
test_union_cast-1_safe.cil.c	safe	0.01	error	0.05	safe	0.06	safe	0.02	safe	0.06
test_union_cast-2_safe.c	safe	0.01	error	0.06	safe	0.05	safe	0.02	safe	0.07
test_union_cast-2_safe.cil.c	safe	0.01	error	0.06	safe	0.04	safe	0.02	safe	0.09
test_union_cast.c_safe_1.cil.c	safe	0.01	error	0.05	safe	0.04	safe	0.02	safe	0.09
test_union_cast.c_safe.cil.c	safe	0.01	error	0.05	safe	0.04	safe	0.03	safe	0.08

test_union.c_safe_1.cil.c	unsafe	0.03	safe	0.35	safe	0.04	safe	0.01	safe	0.07
test_union.c_safe.cil.c	safe	0.02	safe	0.21	safe	0.04	safe	0.01	safe	0.07
test_while_int.c_unsafe_1.cil.c	unsafe	0.8	unsafe	0.47	unsafe	0.06	unsafe	0.02	unsafe	0.04
test_while_int.c_unsafe.cil.c	unsafe	0.96	safe	0.29	unsafe	0.05	unsafe	0.03	unsafe	0.04
volatile_alias.c_safe_1.cil.c	safe	0.02	safe	0.2	safe	0.04	safe	0.01	safe	0.08
volatile_alias.c_safe.cil.c	safe	0.03	safe	0.2	safe	0.04	safe	0.01	safe	0.08
1_3.c_unsafe.i	unsafe	0.05	unsafe	0.29	unsafe	0.05	unsafe	0.03	unsafe	0.11
alias_of_return_2.c_safe_1.i	safe	0.02	safe	0.13	safe	0.05	safe	0.02	safe	0.07
alias_of_return_2.c_safe.i	safe	0.01	safe	0.14	safe	0.04	safe	0.02	safe	0.09
alias_of_return.c_safe_1.i	safe	0.01	safe	0.24	safe	0.05	safe	0.02	safe	0.09
alias_of_return.c_safe.i	safe	0.01	safe	0.25	safe	0.04	safe	0.02	safe	0.09
alt_test.c_unsafe.i	unsafe	1.25	unsafe	0.45	unsafe	0.07	unsafe	0.07	unsafe	0.04
callfpointer.c_unsafe.i	unsafe	0.04	error	0.06	unsafe	0.04	unsafe	0.02	unsafe	0.04
ex3_forlist.c_safe.i	error	114.21	safe	0.17	safe	0.07	safe	0.04	safe	0.17
fo_test.c_unsafe.i	unsafe	0.05	unsafe	0.49	unsafe	0.09	unsafe	0.06	unsafe	0.05
just_assert.c_safe.i	safe	0.02	safe	0.13	safe	0.04	safe	0.01	safe	0.07
mutex_lock_int.c_safe_1.i	safe	0.01	safe	0.15	safe	0.04	safe	0.02	safe	0.07
mutex_lock_int.c_unsafe.i	unsafe	0.03	unsafe	0.3	unsafe	0.04	unsafe	0.02	unsafe	0.04
mutex_lock_struct.c_safe_1.i	safe	0.02	safe	0.15	safe	0.04	safe	0.02	safe	0.06
mutex_lock_struct.c_unsafe.i	unsafe	0.03	unsafe	0.15	unsafe	0.04	unsafe	0.03	unsafe	0.04
nested_structure.c_safe.i	safe	0.02	safe	0.13	safe	0.04	safe	0.04	safe	0.08
nested_structure_noptr.c_safe.i	safe	0.01	safe	0.13	safe	0.04	safe	0.02	safe	0.06
nested_structure_noptr_safe.i	safe	0.01	safe	0.14	safe	0.04	safe	0.04	safe	0.07
nested_structure_ptr.c_safe.i	safe	0.02	safe	0.34	safe	0.04	safe	0.02	safe	0.08
nested_structure_ptr_safe.i	safe	0.01	safe	0.14	safe	0.05	safe	0.02	safe	0.08
nested_structure_safe.i	safe	0.01	safe	0.15	safe	0.04	safe	0.02	safe	0.1
oomInt.c_safe_1.i	safe	0.01	safe	0.14	safe	0.05	safe	0.02	safe	0.09
oomInt.c_safe.i	safe	0.01	safe	0.4	safe	0.05	safe	0.02	safe	0.06
recursive_list.c_unsafe.i	unsafe	0.08	unsafe	0.3	unsafe	0.05	unsafe	0.03	unknown	0.06
rule57_ebda_blast.c_safe_1.i	safe	1.2	safe	0.17	safe	0.06	safe	0.05	safe	0.38
rule57_ebda_blast.c_unsafe.i	unsafe	0.05	unsafe	0.17	unsafe	0.06	unsafe	0.05	unsafe	0.18
rule60_list2.c_safe.i	safe	3.26	safe	0.4	safe	0.07	safe	0.06	safe	0.1
rule60_list2.c_unsafe_1.i	unsafe	3.37	unsafe	0.54	unsafe	0.07	unsafe	0.1	unsafe	0.05
rule60_list.c_safe.i	safe	0.03	safe	0.39	safe	0.06	safe	0.05	safe	0.35
sizeofparameters_test.c_safe.i	unsafe	0.03	unsafe	0.37	safe	0.06	safe	0.03	unsafe	0.04
stateful_check_unsafe.i	unsafe	1.11	unsafe	0.93	unsafe	0.25	unsafe	41.66	unsafe	0.04
structure_assignment.c_safe.i	safe	0.01	safe	0.14	safe	0.04	safe	0.02	safe	0.06
test_address.c_safe.i	unsafe	0.04	safe	0.38	safe	0.06	safe	0.04	safe	0.08
test_cut_trace.c_safe.i	safe	0.03	safe	0.14	safe	0.04	safe	0.02	safe	0.09
test_malloc-1_safe.i	unsafe	0.04	safe	0.39	safe	0.06	safe	0.05	safe	0.25
test_malloc-2_safe.i	unsafe	0.05	safe	0.39	safe	0.06	safe	0.06	safe	0.05
test_overflow.c_safe.i	unsafe	0.05	unsafe	0.44	safe	0.09	safe	0.06	unsafe	0.09
test_union_cast-1_safe.i	safe	0.02	error	0.13	safe	0.04	safe	0.02	safe	0.08
test_union_cast-2_safe.i	safe	0.01	error	0.04	safe	0.04	safe	0.02	safe	0.08
test_union_cast.c_safe_1.i	safe	0.01	error	0.05	safe	0.05	safe	0.02	safe	0.1
test_union_cast.c_safe.i	safe	0.03	error	0.05	safe	0.04	safe	0.02	safe	0.1
test_union.c_safe_1.i	unsafe	0.03	safe	0.16	safe	0.04	safe	0.02	safe	0.07
test_union.c_safe.i	safe	0.02	safe	0.14	safe	0.05	safe	0.02	safe	0.09
test_while_int.c_unsafe_1.i	unsafe	0.82	unsafe	0.29	unsafe	0.04	unsafe	0.03	unsafe	0.04
test_while_int.c_unsafe.i	unsafe	1.03	unsafe	16.02	unsafe	0.04	unsafe	0.03	unsafe	0.05
volatile_alias.c_safe_1.i	safe	0.02	safe	0.14	safe	0.04	safe	0.02	safe	0.08
volatile_alias.c_safe.i	safe	0.01	safe	0.14	safe	0.04	safe	0.05	safe	0.26

Loops The loop category of the SV-Comp13 covers all kinds of different benchmarks. Each benchmark contains at least one loop. The complexity in this category is reached by having the calls to the error label hidden somewhere inside the loop. The deeper this call is inside a loop and in addition with the connection to some conditions, the more complex the problem is.

Figure 4.3 shows the performance of the tools regarding runtime and Figure 4.4 shows the comparison regarding memory consumption.

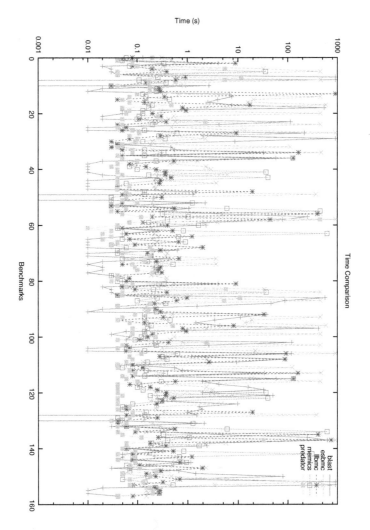

Figure 4.3. Performance Comparison between MEMICS and several State of the Art Tools for the Category Loops: Runtime

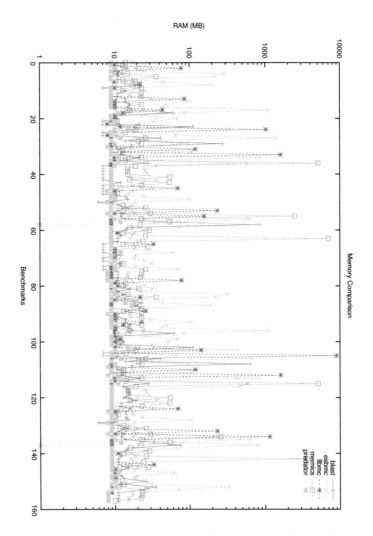

Figure 4.4. Performance Comparison between MEMICS and several State of the Art Tools for the Category Loops: Memory Consumption

In terms of runtime, MEMICS competes quite well and is in almost any benchmark at least in average time. Only in a very few cases is MEMICS the tool with the longest runtime. The same results are observable from the memory consumption graph.

Again, the timing and memory results are not the actual relevant comparison criteria. This is the percentage of benchmarks checked with the correct result, which is shown in Table 4.3. The winner in this category is LLBMC, followed by ESBMC and MEMICS achieves the third place.

Table 4.3. Overall Results of the Category Loops from the Software Verification Competition 2013

	blast	esbmc	llbmc	memics	predator
Score (%):	58.86	91.77	92.41	74.68	60.75
Time (s):	8597.04	13366.28	3426.0	2517.21	540.34

The detailed results of this category are shown in Table 4.4, where the first block contains the pure C source files and the second block contains preprocessed source code of the same benchmarks.

Table 4.4. Detailed Results of the Category Loops from the Software Verification Competition 2013

Benchmark	blast		esbmc		llbmc		memics		Predator	
	Result	Time	Result	Time	Result	Time	Result	Time	Result	Time
array_safe.c	unsafe	0.13	safe	0.31	safe	0.08	safe	0.06	unsafe	0.2
array_unsafe.c	unsafe	0.05	unsafe	0.48	unsafe	0.04	unsafe	0.05	unsafe	0.04
bist.cell_safe.c	safe	4.05	safe	0.58	safe	8.84	safe	0.34	safe	0.08
bubble_sort_safe.c	safe	0.02	safe	0.33	safe	0.08	safe	0.07	unknown	0.1
bubble_sort_unsafe.c	error	0.03	error	32.42	unsafe	0.2	unsafe	0.2	unknown	5.47
count_up_down_safe.c	unsafe	0.03	unsafe	450.2	safe	0.39	safe	35.66	unsafe	0.04
count_up_down_unsafe.c	unsafe	0.04	unsafe	0.19	unsafe	0.04	unsafe	0.04	unsafe	0.04
eureka_01_safe.c	timeout	910.0	safe	0.61	safe	0.92	safe	0.26	safe	11.53
eureka_01_unsafe.c	timeout	910.0	unsafe	454.6	unsafe	0.59	safe	0.11	unknown	5.43
eureka_05_safe.c	error	0.0	safe	0.56	safe	0.15	safe	0.38	safe	0.17
for_bounded_loop1_unsafe.c	unsafe	2.67	unsafe	0.86	unsafe	0.03	unsafe	0.03	unsafe	0.04
for_infinite_loop_1_safe.c	safe	0.02	safe	0.25	safe	0.28	safe	0.25	safe	0.18
for_infinite_loop_2_safe.c	safe	0.01	safe	0.26	safe	0.29	safe	0.24	safe	0.18
insertion_sort_safe.c	unsafe	6.78	safe	0.68	timeout	910.0	error	0.13	unknown	0.1
insertion_sort_unsafe.c	unsafe	7.5	unsafe	450.47	unsafe	0.35	error	0.15	unknown	0.07
invert_string_safe.c	unsafe	3.97	safe	20.68	safe	0.04	safe	0.44	unknown	0.05
invert_string_unsafe.c	unsafe	2.54	unsafe	15.73	unsafe	0.14	error	0.15	unknown	0.07
kundu_safe.c	error	7.53	safe	583.83	error	17.26	safe	0.2	safe	0.48
kundu_unsafe.c	unsafe	538.13	unsafe	2.46	unsafe	0.8	safe	0.17	unsafe	0.05
linear_sea.ch_safe.c	unsafe	0.05	safe	0.3	safe	0.94	error	0.13	unknown	0.07
linear_search_unsafe.c	unsafe	0.05	safe	450.19	unsafe	0.2	error	0.13	unknown	0.06
list_safe.c	error	0.02	safe	0.54	error	0.3	safe	0.11	safe	0.26
list_unsafe.c	error	0.02	unsafe	0.42	error	0.11	unsafe	0.1	unsafe	0.05
lu.cmp_safe.c	safe	112.94	safe	0.58	safe	0.38	safe	0.23	safe	2.28

91

4. Tests and Results

File										
ludcmp_unsafe.c	unsafe	4.21	unsafe	450.86	unsafe	0.04	unsafe	0.2	unsafe	0.05
matrix_safe.c	error	0.01	safe	0.48	safe	0.06	safe	0.05	unsafe	0.04
matrix_unsafe.c	error	0.01	unsafe	13.38	unsafe	0.05	error	0.14	unknown	0.08
mem_slave_tlm_safe.c	safe	215.34	timeout	910.0	error	9.21	safe	0.62	safe	0.11
n.c11_safe.c	safe	2.05	safe	0.4	safe	0.29	safe	0.27	safe	0.07
n.c24_safe.c	timeout	910.0	error	2.27	error	0.07	safe	0.36	unknown	0.1
n.c40_safe.c	error	8.62	safe	0.2	safe	0.03	error	0.13	safe	0.09
nec11_unsafe.c	unsafe	0.04	unsafe	0.18	unsafe	0.04	unsafe	0.04	unsafe	0.05
nec20_unsafe.c	unsafe	0.47	unsafe	111.9	unsafe	0.03	unsafe	0.05	unknown	0.04
nec40_safe.c	unsafe	0.56	safe	0.2	safe	0.05	error	0.14	safe	0.08
pc_sfifo_1_safe.c	safe	32.55	safe	466.98	safe	164.52	safe	0.34	unsafe	0.08
pc_sfifo_2_unsafe.c	unsafe	0.05	unsafe	0.29	unsafe	0.05	unsafe	0.14	unsafe	0.04
s3_unsafe.c	unsafe	57.42	safe	18.42	unsafe	128.39	safe	126.37	unknown	0.05
string_safe.c	error	0.02	safe	1.59	safe	0.54	safe	0.24	safe	0.1
string_unsafe.c	error	0.01	unsafe	0.45	unsafe	0.07	unsafe	0.09	unknown	0.04
sum01_bug02_sum01_bug02_base.case_-unsafe.c	error	0.01	unsafe	2.34	unsafe	0.15	unsafe	0.07	unsafe	0.03
sum01_bug02_unsafe.c	error	0.01	unsafe	2.92	unsafe	0.24	unsafe	0.1	unsafe	0.04
sum01_safe.c	error	0.01	safe	0.24	safe	0.37	safe	36.44	unsafe	0.04
sum01_unsafe.c	error	0.02	unsafe	6.15	unsafe	0.36	unsafe	0.17	unsafe	0.05
sum02_safe.c	error	0.25	safe	0.27	safe	0.48	safe	40.0	unsafe	0.04
sum03_safe.c	error	0.01	safe	0.22	safe	0.29	safe	0.25	unsafe	0.04
sum03_unsafe.c	error	0.01	unsafe	3.72	unsafe	0.28	unsafe	0.06	unsafe	0.04
sum04_safe.c	error	0.01	safe	0.22	safe	0.04	safe	0.04	safe	0.07
sum04_unsafe.c	error	0.01	unsafe	0.23	unsafe	0.04	unsafe	0.04	unsafe	0.04
sum_array_safe.c	unsafe	1.47	safe	0.35	safe	19.43	error	0.14	unknown	0.06
sum_array_unsafe.c	unsafe	1.29	unsafe	369.46	unsafe	0.05	error	0.14	unknown	0.07
terminator_01_safe.c	error	0.0	safe	0.23	safe	0.31	safe	0.03	safe	0.06
terminator_01_unsafe.c	unsafe	0.03	unsafe	0.21	unsafe	0.05	unsafe	0.03	unsafe	0.05
terminator_02_safe.c	safe	2.26	safe	0.2	safe	0.05	safe	1.25	safe	0.1
terminator_02_unsafe.c	unsafe	0.05	unsafe	0.21	unsafe	0.03	unsafe	0.03	unsafe	0.04
terminator_03_safe.c	safe	1.07	safe	0.26	safe	0.55	safe	6.01	safe	0.06
terminator_03_unsafe.c	unsafe	0.29	unsafe	0.2	unsafe	0.04	error	448.0	unsafe	0.03
token_ring01_safe.c	safe	4.84	safe	456.0	safe	394.28	safe	0.32	unsafe	0.05
token_ring01_unsafe.c	unsafe	248.61	unsafe	0.86	unsafe	0.2	safe	1.04	unsafe	0.12
toy_safe.c	error	79.0	timeout	910.0	error	44.04	safe	0.4	error	447.0
transmitter_unsafe.c	unsafe	2.02	unsafe	3.92	unsafe	0.13	unsafe	0.17	unsafe	0.07
trex01_safe.c	safe	2.34	safe	0.31	safe	0.4	safe	1.66	unsafe	0.04
trex01_unsafe.c	unsafe	0.04	unsafe	0.19	unsafe	0.05	unsafe	0.04	unsafe	0.01
trex02_safe.c	safe	0.26	safe	0.24	safe	0.51	safe	0.83	safe	0.03
trex02_unsafe.c	unsafe	0.05	unsafe	0.22	unsafe	0.06	safe	620.41	unsafe	0.02
trex03_safe.c	unsafe	0.05	safe	0.27	safe	1.23	safe	0.66	safe	0.03
trex03_unsafe.c	error	0.01	unsafe	0.2	unsafe	0.07	unsafe	0.05	unsafe	0.02
trex04_safe.c	error	0.01	safe	0.25	safe	0.67	safe	0.91	safe	0.04
veris.c_NetBSD-libc__loop_safe.c	error	0.01	safe	0.22	safe	0.09	safe	0.03	safe	0.03
veris.c_OpenSER__cases1_stripFullBoth_-arr_safe.c	error	0.01	safe	1.85	safe	2.01	safe	0.06	unknown	0.18
veris.c_sendmail__tTflag_arr_one_loop_-safe.c	safe	0.63	safe	0.34	safe	0.29	safe	0.29	unknown	0.2
verisec_NetBSD-libc__loop_unsafe.c	error	0.01	unsafe	0.4	unsafe	0.16	unsafe	0.04	unsafe	0.05
verisec_OpenSER_cases1_stripFullBoth_-arr_unsafe.c	error	0.01	unsafe	0.37	unsafe	0.19	error	0.19	unknown	0.18
verisec_sendmail__tTflag_arr_one_loop_-unsafe.c	safe	0.43	unsafe	3.67	unsafe	0.68	safe	0.05	unsafe	0.08
vogal_safe.c	error	0.02	safe	0.27	safe	0.24	error	0.16	unknown	0.14
vogal_unsafe.c	error	0.01	unsafe	3.67	unsafe	0.05	error	0.52	unsafe	0.08
while_infinite_loop_1_safe.c	safe	0.02	safe	0.21	safe	0.29	safe	0.24	safe	0.09
while_infinite_loop_2_safe.c	safe	0.02	safe	0.22	safe	0.27	safe	0.24	safe	0.1
while_infinite_loop_3_safe.c	safe	0.01	safe	0.21	safe	0.31	safe	0.26	safe	0.2
while_infinite_loop_4_unsafe.c	unsafe	0.03	unsafe	0.19	unsafe	0.04	unsafe	0.03	unsafe	0.04
array_safe.i	unsafe	0.05	safe	0.39	safe	0.07	safe	0.04	unsafe	0.04
array_unsafe.i	unsafe	0.05	unsafe	0.38	unsafe	0.06	unsafe	0.04	unsafe	0.03
bist.cell_safe.i	safe	4.01	safe	0.57	safe	9.01	safe	0.34	safe	0.08
bubble_sort_safe.i	safe	0.02	safe	0.26	safe	0.05	safe	0.05	unknown	0.06
bubble_sort_unsafe.i	error	0.03	unsafe	33.57	unsafe	0.09	unsafe	0.21	unknown	5.72
count_up_down_safe.i	unsafe	0.03	unsafe	450.18	safe	0.39	safe	36.66	unsafe	0.05
count_up_down_unsafe.i	unsafe	0.04	unsafe	0.14	unsafe	0.04	unsafe	0.04	unsafe	0.05
eureka_01_safe.i	error	561.03	safe	0.54	safe	0.98	safe	0.25	safe	10.87
eureka_01_unsafe.i	error	87.0	unsafe	454.47	unsafe	0.61	safe	0.1	unknown	5.27
eureka_05_safe.i	error	45.8	safe	0.39	safe	0.22	safe	0.37	safe	0.18

92

for_bounded_loop1_unsafe.i	unsafe	1.55	unsafe	0.15	unsafe	0.04	unsafe	0.04	unsafe	0.04
for_infinite_loop_1_safe.i	safe	0.02	safe	0.14	safe	0.23	safe	0.24	safe	0.17
for_infinite_loop_2_safe.i	safe	0.01	safe	0.14	safe	0.29	safe	0.24	safe	0.16
insertion_sort_safe.i	unsafe	37.36	safe	0.5	error	33.15	error	0.14	unknown	0.09
insertion_sort_unsafe.i	unsafe	11.15	unsafe	450.37	unsafe	0.33	error	0.14	unknown	0.05
invert_string_safe.i	unsafe	3.45	safe	19.05	safe	0.04	safe	0.45	unknown	0.04
invert_string_unsafe.i	unsafe	1.46	unsafe	13.68	unsafe	0.14	error	0.15	unknown	0.07
kundu_safe.i	error	4.32	safe	585.96	error	8.1	safe	0.19	safe	0.51
kundu_unsafe.i	unsafe	414.55	unsafe	2.37	unsafe	0.8	safe	0.16	unsafe	0.08
linear_search_safe.i	unsafe	0.06	safe	0.24	safe	0.94	error	0.14	unknown	0.08
linear_search_unsafe.i	unsafe	0.03	safe	450.19	unsafe	0.2	error	0.14	unknown	0.08
list_safe.i	unsafe	0.07	safe	0.54	safe	0.16	safe	0.12	safe	0.23
list_unsafe.i	unsafe	0.06	unsafe	0.45	unsafe	0.11	unsafe	0.09	unsafe	0.04
lu.cmp_safe.i	safe	119.41	safe	0.81	safe	0.42	safe	0.23	safe	2.32
ludcmp_unsafe.i	unsafe	2.64	unsafe	451.18	unsafe	0.06	unsafe	0.24	unsafe	0.05
matrix_safe.i	error	0.01	safe	0.31	safe	0.07	safe	0.06	unsafe	0.04
matrix_unsafe.i	error	0.01	unsafe	22.21	unsafe	0.06	error	0.14	unknown	0.07
mem_slave_tlm_safe.i	safe	117.7	timeout	910.0	error	92.17	safe	0.63	safe	0.12
n.c11_safe.i	safe	1.21	safe	0.35	safe	0.28	safe	0.31	safe	0.07
n.c24_safe.i	error	91.0	error	2.4	unknown	87.0	safe	0.39	unknown	0.08
n.c40_safe.i	error	9.27	safe	0.13	safe	2.66	error	0.16	safe	0.06
nec11_unsafe.i	unsafe	0.06	unsafe	0.16	unsafe	0.08	unsafe	0.04	unsafe	0.04
nec20_unsafe.i	unsafe	0.55	unsafe	122.6	unsafe	0.13	unsafe	0.05	unknown	0.04
nec40_safe.i	unsafe	0.78	safe	0.17	safe	0.08	error	0.15	safe	0.07
pc_sfifo_1_safe.i	safe	33.67	safe	467.35	safe	159.72	safe	0.36	unsafe	0.09
pc_sfifo_2_unsafe.i	unsafe	0.08	unsafe	0.28	unsafe	0.08	unsafe	0.14	unsafe	0.05
s3_unsafe.i	unsafe	57.82	safe	18.68	unsafe	129.62	safe	129.65	unknown	0.06
string_safe.i	safe	1.97	safe	450.25	safe	0.57	safe	0.3	unknown	0.1
string_unsafe.i	unsafe	4.12	unsafe	0.38	unsafe	0.07	unsafe	0.11	unknown	0.04
sum01_bug02_sum01_bug02_base.case_-unsafe.i	unsafe	15.83	unsafe	2.35	unsafe	0.18	unsafe	0.1	unsafe	0.04
sum01_bug02_unsafe.i	unsafe	32.5	unsafe	3.13	unsafe	0.25	unsafe	0.13	unsafe	0.04
sum01_safe.i	safe	1.98	safe	0.23	safe	0.38	safe	36.29	unsafe	0.04
sum01_unsafe.i	unsafe	49.58	unsafe	7.77	unsafe	0.36	unsafe	0.18	unsafe	0.05
sum02_safe.i	error	0.25	safe	0.25	safe	0.53	safe	39.36	unsafe	0.04
sum03_safe.i	safe	0.33	safe	0.18	safe	0.31	safe	0.29	unsafe	0.04
sum03_unsafe.i	unsafe	9.71	unsafe	4.56	unsafe	0.24	unsafe	0.08	unsafe	0.04
sum04_safe.i	safe	1.69	safe	0.24	safe	0.06	safe	0.05	safe	0.07
sum04_unsafe.i	unsafe	1.93	unsafe	0.24	unsafe	0.06	unsafe	0.05	unsafe	0.04
sum_array_safe.i	unsafe	0.98	safe	0.34	safe	19.49	error	0.15	unknown	0.08
sum_array_unsafe.i	unsafe	1.52	unsafe	378.05	unsafe	0.06	error	0.14	unknown	0.08
terminator_01_safe.i	error	0.0	safe	0.16	safe	0.25	safe	0.04	safe	0.07
terminator_01_unsafe.i	unsafe	0.05	unsafe	0.13	unsafe	0.04	unsafe	0.05	unsafe	0.03
terminator_02_safe.i	safe	2.12	safe	0.2	safe	0.04	safe	1.27	safe	0.06
terminator_02_unsafe.i	unsafe	0.03	unsafe	0.28	unsafe	0.06	unsafe	0.06	unsafe	0.04
terminator_03_safe.i	safe	0.56	safe	0.55	safe	0.56	safe	5.98	safe	0.1
terminator_03_unsafe.i	unsafe	0.29	unsafe	0.15	unsafe	0.09	error	616.71	unsafe	0.04
token_ring01_safe.i	safe	4.88	safe	455.99	safe	404.87	safe	0.33	unsafe	0.05
token_ring01_unsafe.i	unsafe	245.51	unsafe	0.82	unsafe	0.26	safe	1.07	unsafe	0.12
toy_safe.i	error	623.1	timeout	910.0	error	746.0	safe	0.4	error	32.2
transmitter_unsafe.i	unsafe	2.16	unsafe	5.63	unsafe	0.18	unsafe	0.19	unsafe	0.06
trex01_safe.i	safe	2.4	safe	0.29	safe	0.37	safe	1.68	unsafe	0.06
trex01_unsafe.i	unsafe	0.07	unsafe	0.17	unsafe	0.06	unsafe	0.06	unsafe	0.05
trex02_safe.i	safe	0.32	safe	0.2	safe	0.52	safe	0.83	safe	0.09
trex02_unsafe.i	unsafe	0.05	unsafe	0.16	unsafe	0.08	error	304.88	unsafe	0.04
trex03_safe.i	unsafe	0.05	safe	0.22	safe	1.21	safe	0.68	safe	0.09
trex03_unsafe.i	unsafe	0.04	unsafe	0.8	unsafe	0.08	unsafe	0.08	unsafe	0.04
trex04_safe.i	safe	1.15	safe	0.56	safe	0.7	safe	0.94	safe	0.09
veris.c_NetBSD-libc__loop_safe.i	safe	0.48	safe	0.16	safe	0.11	safe	0.06	safe	0.07
veris.c_OpenSER__cases1_stripFullBoth_-arr_safe.i	safe	0.03	safe	2.3	safe	1.96	safe	0.07	unknown	0.11
veris.c_sendmail__tTflag_arr_one_loop_-safe.i	safe	0.66	safe	0.41	safe	0.29	safe	0.07	unknown	0.24
verisec_NetBSD-libc__loop_unsafe.i	unsafe	1.43	unsafe	0.22	unsafe	0.15	unsafe	0.05	unsafe	0.05
verisec_OpenSER__cases1_stripFullBoth_-arr_unsafe.i	unsafe	79.07	unsafe	0.47	unsafe	0.23	error	0.16	unknown	0.18
verisec_sendmail__tTflag_arr_one_loop_-unsafe.i	safe	0.58	unsafe	6.16	unsafe	0.69	safe	0.05	unsafe	0.07
vogal_safe.i	timeout	910.0	safe	450.31	safe	0.32	error	0.14	unknown	0.13
vogal_unsafe.i	timeout	910.0	unsafe	3.42	unsafe	0.08	error	0.51	unsafe	0.07

while_infinite_loop_1_safe.i	safe	0.02	safe	0.15	safe	0.22	safe	0.23	safe	0.18
while_infinite_loop_2_safe.i	safe	0.01	safe	0.15	safe	0.28	safe	0.23	safe	0.2
while_infinite_loop_3_safe.i	safe	0.01	safe	0.16	safe	0.27	safe	0.27	safe	0.2
while_infinite_loop_4_unsafe.i	unsafe	0.04	unsafe	0.15	unsafe	0.08	unsafe	0.04	unsafe	0.04

While this result is already good for a proof-of-concept implementation, one thing has to be mentioned regarding the remaining benchmarks, which MEMICS was not able to verify successfully. The benchmarks: insertion_sort*, invert_string*, linear_search*, matrix_unsafe, sum_array*, and verisec_-sendmail contain at least one dynamic array, which is constructed based on an undefined, unsigned integer value. Since MEMICS is working based on intervals, this requires the allocation of an array of size $[0, 2^{32} - 1]$. This is currently not supported, because it leads to a huge memory consumption in MEMICS and can possibly influence its stability. In the future however, MEMICS is going to be able to deal with dynamic arrays, but they will have to be defined on proper bounds – i. e., using assumptions for the bounds. The benchmarks nec40_safe* and n.c_safe* both contain uninitialized arrays of fixed size. In both cases one of these arrays is accessed under the condition while (array[i++] != 0). Since the array is uninitialized it can be possible that there exists a 0 inside the array. But on the other hand, it is not guaranteed, which results in an index out of bounds access to the array. MEMICS terminates exactly with the identification of this error, because the main purpose of MEMICS is the discovery of any runtime error.

4.2 The Automotive Race Condition Example

In this section MEMICS is applied to the running automotive race condition Example 2.3.1. In Figure 4.5 the result of a run is shown, where the number of pixels has been set to 500.

The runtime error identified by MEMICS is exactly the race condition (lost update) between the computation of the Laplace Operator for the first pixel and the update of the last pixel from the internal image buffer. For the entire operation, MEMICS is running about half an hour. Though, this might sound long, it states that the current proof-of-concept implementation of MEMICS is very stable.

```
user@memics:~/$ memics automotive-example.c -c automotive-example.conf
Model is Unsafe

Runtime error: lost update
  thrown from task/thread: readInputs
  present in file: /home/user/automotive-example.c @ line 31
    sensor_values[i] = readSensors(i);
                       ^
  in conflict with task/thread: worker1
  present in file: /home/user/automotive-example.c @ line 49
    tmp[i] = sensors[left(i, NUM_SENSORS)] - 2*sensors[i] + sensors[right(i, NUM_SENSORS)];
             ^
```

Figure 4.5. The Result Output of MEMICS after Solving the Automotive Example 2.3.1

To properly test MEMICS on scalability, using the automotive example, the number of pixels (sensors) has been varied from 3 up to 2000. Figure 4.6 shows the results of MEMICS for the first 500 benchmarks. The overall runtime in

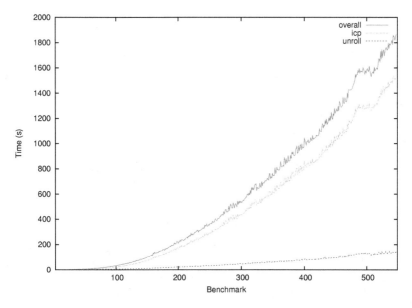

Figure 4.6. Performance of MEMICS for the Automotive Example: Runtime

this chart is represented by the overall (red) curve. This curve is divided into the two curves: icp (green) and unrolling (blue). The results show that the overall time consumed by MEMICS increases superlinearly. Where the time for unrolling increases linearly and is quite small, the time spent on icp also increases superlinearly. As aforementioned in Chapter 3, the solver spends most of its time on icp. The remaining parts used in MEMICS are so small time-wise, that they are not shown here.

The memory consumption of MEMICS, in contrast to the runtime, is increasing linearly. The reason therefore is that from benchmark to benchmark exactly one run of the Laplace operator is added, which therefore already is linear.

4.3   Results

The tests presented in this chapter have shown that MEMICS is running reliably. In addition it has been shown that MEMICS is able to correctly identify the runtime errors presented in Table 2.3. Even on benchmarks, where MEMICS has to run for over one hour, it does not segfault and still obtains the correct result. Although the results also show that MEMICS can be used on industrial software, its overall performance regarding runtime will not be very good. On the other hand, since MEMICS is still limited to the state explosion problem – like any other formal verification tool – it will require the latest hardware in terms of physical memory and CPU technology.

Concurrency Issues from SV-Comp13   There exists a category called concurrency issues at the SV-Comp13, although all provided test cases are implemented on the base of POSIX Threads (pthreads) [91]. In an early version of MEMICS, which was used to retrieve the result published in [84], pthreads have been properly implemented and were working. But, due to a major rework of MEMICS, the current implementation does not feature pthreads. On the other hand, the verification goal for the concurrency benchmarks, again, is the reachability of the label "ERROR" without taking care about any possible race condition. Hence, even if MEMICS would support pthreads, it will in most of the cases straight forwardly identify a race condition and therefore not reach the requested error location.

The aforementioned state explosion problem is inherent to formal verification tools. A possible trade-off therefore is the combination of "fast" tools using approximate techniques and "slow" tools providing very precise results. In the following Chapter such combinations are introduced and it shows how MEMICS can be used in an industrial tool chain to obtain the best and most precise results.

Chapter 5

Workflow

An example for the current process of static software analysis in the automotive domain, as recommended by the ISO 26262, is shown in Figure 5.1. In this

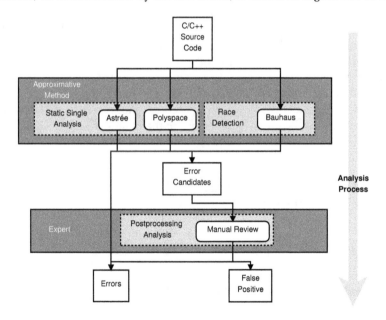

Figure 5.1. Example Process of Static Software Analysis in the Automotive Domain

process C/C++ source is analyzed by static software analysis tools like Astrée,

Polyspace or many others, and e. g., the race detection tool Bauhaus. As stated in Chapter 2, these tools are able to handle large amounts of source code, because all of them work with approximative techniques. However, they all suffer from imprecision in their results. Therefore, the output of these tools includes two categories:

1. Runtime errors the tool can explicitly identify, and

2. Error candidates, where the tool can not decide, if the error holds or not.

The number of error candidates can be very large, especially in terms of concurrent errors. The reason for that is based on the fact that each possible pair of read-write or write-write correlations is reported as a race condition. Therefore, it is obvious that this number can be huge in terms of industrial software consisting of up to several million lines of code.

In order to filter the error candidates into real runtime errors and false positives, a manual review is required. This review has to be made by an expert in C/C++ source code, and is in most of the cases very expensive in terms of time. Therefore, the reviewer usually only checks those errors with the highest severity for risk of failure. When it comes to the manual review of concurrent runtime errors, it is much more difficult to decide whether an error candidate is a real error or just a false positive.

In the following section, the combination of industrial tools with the MEMICS software verification tool is introduced.

5.1 Tool-Chain of Static Software Analysis Tools

The tool-chain in which MEMICS can be embedded is shown in Figure 5.2. In this workflow MEMICS is used to verify, which of the error candidates are real errors and which are false positives. There exist several possible scenarios on the combination of static software analysis tools, since in general there exist many more tools in the approximative category. In the following, two scenarios, representing each category, are introduced and discussed in detail: in Section 5.2 the combination of MEMICS and Polyspace and in Section 5.3 the combination of Bauhaus and MEMICS.

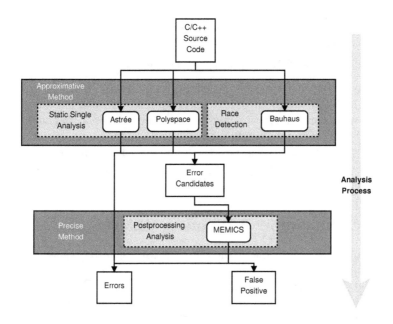

Figure 5.2. The new Workflow – Using MEMICS as the Postprocessing Engine

5.2 Combination: MEMICS ↔ Polyspace

The general result of a Polyspace analysis is divided into 5 different groups: green, red, orange, grey and purple. The green group contains good code and the red identified runtime errors. In the orange group the unproven errors are gathered. The grey group contains dead or unreachable code and the purple group indicates code rule violations. Hence, the most critical group is the orange one – the error candidates –, since Polyspace is not able to verify its content.

Let's assume Polyspace identifies a potential division by zero in line 34 of file A, where the dividend is x. In general a manual reviewer has to decide whether x can really be equal to zero at that certain point or not. But, one can also use

MEMICS to retrieve that information. The relevant target question MEMICS
requires to verify the property looks like:

$$\mathtt{loc} = \mathtt{PC(A:34)} \wedge \mathtt{reg(loc:}x) = 0$$

With the help of the MEMICS internal mapping between input source code
and the MEMICS model, the pattern PC(filename:linenumber) computes the
actual program counter for the relevant assembly instruction. In addition the
pattern reg(location:variable) retrieves the corresponding register for the
current variable – also using the same map. The solver then has to checked
whether there exists any path leading to the location of the variable x and if the
corresponding register contains the value 0.

5.3 Combination: Bauhaus ↔ MEMICS

In the combination of Bauhaus and MEMICS two scenarios have to be considered. In the first case MEMICS is used to check, which of the detected race pairs
are valid in the current system, or not. Such a race pair is in general defined
by the access to one global resource from two different tasks A and B. The conflicting access can either be of type: read/write or write/write. It is possible that
depending on the level of approximation Bauhaus can not determine the exact
source location for those two accesses. In such a case, a manual review can be
really hard and even almost impossible, since there may exist more than one
access to the conflicting resource from both tasks. Hence, a tool like MEMICS is
required to analyze such problems.

Let's assume Bauhaus detected a race pair between the two tasks A and B for
the global resource x. The target question for MEMICS in order to verify the
property is defined as:

$$\mathtt{clk(load,\ A,\ }x) > \mathtt{clk(write,\ B,\ }x)$$

With this information, MEMICS searches for all read access from task A as well as
all write access from task B to the resource x and checks, if for one pair out of all
interleavings the read access occurs after the write access. In case Bauhaus can
determine the source location of the two conflicting accesses, then the relevant
search space for MEMICS can be reduced considerably. The corresponding target
question is defined as:

$$clk(load, A, x, PC(loc_A)) > clk(write, B, x, PC(loc_B))$$

The second scenario of a combination between Bauhaus and MEMICS is not actually covered by the workflow description in Figure 5.2. It is rather an interaction between both tools, in which Bauhaus uses MEMICS to check, whether a schedule of tasks is valid or not. Let's assume Bauhaus requires the information, if the C statement at file D in line x used from task A and the statement at file E in line y used from task B can occur concurrently under the given scheduling rules in the current system. The target question for MEMICS to check this property is defined as:

$$clk(PC(D{:}x), A) == clk(PC(E{:}y), B).$$

5.4 Results

This chapter has introduced the idea that embedding MEMICS into a tool-chain with industrial static software analysis tools, reduces the effort for expensive manual reviews. On the other hand MEMICS also benefits from these scenarios. As aforementioned in Chapter 4, MEMICS is like any other formal verification tool limited by the state explosion problem. It is therefore possible that MEMICS is not able to detect all the errors identified by the industrial tools on its own. The search for a specific target, only, has almost the same impact as program slicing. In this case the search space is reduced, to those paths leading to the required target, only. Such a possible reduction is shown in Figure 5.3. Depending on the

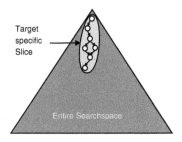

Figure 5.3. MEMICS IR Slice: Search-space Reduction for a specific Target

103

5. Workflow

location of the target, the factor reducing the search space can in some cases be so large that it avoids the state explosion problem.

Chapter 6

Conclusion & Future Work

6.1 Conclusion

The challenge of this thesis was the verification of concurrent embedded software – in particular in the automotive domain. For this reason, the Memory Interval Constraint Solving (MEMICS) software verification approach has been developed as introduced in Chapter 3. MEMICS transforms the input C/C++ source code into the intermediate representation (IR), which is based on the MIPS assembly language. Hence, MEMICS is not working based on any high-level language abstraction. Instead, it uses low-level instructions like those occurring in a real machine. If the system to be checked is an automotive system based on AUTOSAR/OSEK the corresponding system configuration has to be given. In the next step, MEMICS is checking the IR for any kind of runtime error covered in Table 2.3. If MEMICS detects an error, it can return a detailed trace leading to the exact error location.

The implementation of MEMICS has been tested against several others in Chapter 4. The results have shown that the current proof-of-concept implementation of MEMICS is running in a very stable manner and is able to verify systems in the automotive domain. Nevertheless, MEMICS is – like any other formal verification approach – limited by the state explosion problem. In Chapter 5 a limitation of this problem has been described. For this purpose, MEMICS has been embedded into a tool-chain with industrial static software analysis tools. In this chain, MEMICS is used to filter the error candidates – produced by the other tools – into real errors (including a trace to the error) and false positives.

6.2 Future Work

Though, the current work is already very promising, there exist several visions on future work, which could improve the overall performance of MEMICS. These ideas include e. g., the embedding of the CEGAR technique introduced in [54]. With the help of this technique it is possible to create a pre-processing engine for MEMICS, which uses forward- and backward-analysis in order to transfer only the relevant paths for a specific target to MEMICS.

On the other hand it would be very useful, instead of using another tool – e. g., Bauhaus – to gather possible race pairs, to have an embedded frontend dealing with this task. Since MEMICS is already using the LLVM environment, which contains all the relevant information on access to global resources, it could be a moderate effort to implement such an engine.

The third and most generic idea is the MEMICS Module Kit. The current implementation of MEMICS features one verification backend, the internal interval constraint solver, which has been introduced in Section 3.4. The backend is already working well according to the test results from Chapter 4. However, for some analysis types or pre-processing engines as introduced in the ideas above, it is possible that other SMT-Solvers using another theory could be more efficient. For this purpose, the current implementation of the MEMICS Model is as generic as possible. This allows the unrolling procedure to be easily adapted to a various number of SMT theories, which therefore extends MEMICS to almost any available SMT-Solver.

This variability can be very useful, in order to implement pre- and post-processing engines for MEMICS, including e. g., the CEGAR idea from above.

The MEMICS Model for the
Automotive Example 2.3.1

Listing A.1. The MEMICS Model for the Function readSensor from Example 2.3.1 in Chapter 2

```
1   PC = 22 -> PC' = 23;
2   PC = 23 -> PC' = 24;
3   PC = 24 -> sp_reg' = sp_reg +U 4294967280 AND PC' = 25;
4   PC = 25 -> sw(4_reg, memAdr(sp_reg, 12), _clk_) AND PC' = 26;
5   PC = 26 -> lw(2_reg', memAdr(sp_reg, 8), _clk_) AND PC' = 27;
6   PC = 27 -> sw(4_reg, memAdr(sp_reg, 4), _clk_) AND PC' = 28;
7   PC = 28 -> sp_reg' = sp_reg +U 16 AND resetMem(sp_reg, 16) AND
8             PC' = 29;
9   PC = 29 -> PC' = ra_reg;
10  PC = 30 -> PC' = 31;
```

Listing A.2. The MEMICS Model for the Function left from Example 2.3.1 in Chapter 2

```
1   PC = 31 -> PC' = 32;
2   PC = 32 -> PC' = 33;
3   PC = 33 -> sp_reg' = sp_reg +U 4294967280 AND PC' = 34;
4   PC = 34 -> sw(4_reg, memAdr(sp_reg, 12), _clk_) AND PC' = 35;
5   PC = 35 -> sw(5_reg, memAdr(sp_reg, 8), _clk_) AND PC' = 36;
6   PC = 36 -> lw(2_reg', memAdr(sp_reg, 12), _clk_) AND PC' = 37;
7   PC = 37 -> 2_reg' = 2_reg +U 5_reg AND PC' = 38;
8   PC = 38 -> 2_reg' = 2_reg +U 4294967295 AND PC' = 39;
9   PC = 39 -> 3_reg' = 0 +U 5_reg AND PC' = 40;
```

A. The MEMICS Model for the Automotive Example 2.3.1

```
10   PC = 40 -> lo_reg' = 2_reg / 5_reg AND hi_reg' = 2_reg % 5_reg
11               AND PC' = 41;
12   PC = 41 -> 2_reg' = hi_reg AND PC' = 42;
13   PC = 42 -> sw(4_reg, memAdr(sp_reg, 4), _clk_) AND PC' = 43;
14   PC = 43 -> sw(3_reg, memAdr(sp_reg, 0), _clk_) AND PC' = 44;
15   PC = 44 -> sp_reg' = sp_reg +U 16 AND resetMem(sp_reg, 16) AND
16               PC' = 45;
17   PC = 45 -> PC' = ra_reg;
18   PC = 46 -> PC' = 47;
```

Listing A.3. The MEMICS Model for the Function right from Example 2.3.1 in Chapter 2

```
1    PC = 47 -> PC' = 48;
2    PC = 48 -> PC' = 49;
3    PC = 49 -> sp_reg' = sp_reg +U 4294967280 AND PC' = 50;
4    PC = 50 -> sw(4_reg, memAdr(sp_reg, 12), _clk_) AND PC' = 51;
5    PC = 51 -> sw(5_reg, memAdr(sp_reg, 8), _clk_) AND PC' = 52;
6    PC = 52 -> lw(2_reg', memAdr(sp_reg, 12), _clk_) AND PC' = 53;
7    PC = 53 -> 2_reg' = 2_reg +U 1 AND PC' = 54;
8    PC = 54 -> 3_reg' = 0 +U 5_reg AND PC' = 55;
9    PC = 55 -> lo_reg' = 2_reg / 5_reg AND hi_reg' = 2_reg % 5_reg
10               AND PC' = 56;
11   PC = 56 -> 2_reg' = hi_reg AND PC' = 57;
12   PC = 57 -> sw(4_reg, memAdr(sp_reg, 4), _clk_) AND PC' = 58;
13   PC = 58 -> sw(3_reg, memAdr(sp_reg, 0), _clk_) AND PC' = 59;
14   PC = 59 -> sp_reg' = sp_reg +U 16 AND resetMem(sp_reg, 16) AND
15               PC' = 60;
16   PC = 60 -> PC' = ra_reg;
17   PC = 61 -> PC' = 62;
```

Listing A.4. The MEMICS Model for the Function readInputs from Example 2.3.1 in Chapter 2

```
1    PC = 62 -> PC' = 63;
2    PC = 63 -> PC' = 64;
3    PC = 64 -> sp_reg' = sp_reg +U 4294967272 AND PC' = 65;
```

```
 4  PC = 65 -> sw(ra_reg, memAdr(sp_reg, 20), _clk_) AND PC' = 66;
 5  PC = 66 -> 2_reg' = gp_reg +U getGlobalIndex(data1Ready) AND
 6                PC' = 67;
 7  PC = 67 -> lw(4_reg', memAdr(2_reg, 0), _clk_) AND PC' = 68;
 8  PC = 68 -> ra_reg' = 70 AND PC' = 1;
 9  PC = 69 -> PC' = 70;
10  PC = 70 -> 2_reg' = gp_reg +U getGlobalIndex(data2Ready) AND
11                PC' = 71;
12  PC = 71 -> lw(4_reg', memAdr(2_reg, 0), _clk_) AND PC' = 72;
13  PC = 72 -> ra_reg' = 74 AND PC' = 1;
14  PC = 73 -> PC' = 74;
15  PC = 74 -> sw(0, memAdr(sp_reg, 16), _clk_) AND PC' = 75;
16  PC = 75 -> 2_reg' = 0 +U 1 AND PC' = 76;
17  PC = 76 -> lw(3_reg', memAdr(sp_reg, 16), _clk_) AND PC' = 77;
18  PC = 77 -> 2_reg' = 2_reg < 3_reg AND PC' = 78;
19  PC = 78 AND 2_reg != 0 -> PC' = 96;
20  PC = 79 -> PC' = 80;
21  PC = 80 -> PC' = 82;
22  PC = 81 -> PC' = 82;
23  PC = 82 -> lw(4_reg', memAdr(sp_reg, 16), _clk_) AND PC' = 83;
24  PC = 83 -> ra_reg' = 85 AND PC' = 22;
25  PC = 84 -> PC' = 85;
26  PC = 85 -> 4_reg' = gp_reg +U getGlobalIndex(sensors) AND
27                PC' = 86;
28  PC = 86 -> lw(3_reg', memAdr(sp_reg, 16), _clk_) AND PC' = 87;
29  PC = 87 -> lw(4_reg', memAdr(4_reg, 0), _clk_) AND PC' = 88;
30  PC = 88 -> 3_reg' = 3_reg << 2 AND PC' = 89;
31  PC = 89 -> 3_reg' = 4_reg +U 3_reg AND PC' = 90;
32  PC = 90 -> sw(2_reg, memAdr(3_reg, 0), _clk_) AND PC' = 91;
33  PC = 91 -> lw(2_reg', memAdr(sp_reg, 16), _clk_) AND PC' = 92;
34  PC = 92 -> 2_reg' = 2_reg +U 1 AND PC' = 93;
35  PC = 93 -> sw(2_reg, memAdr(sp_reg, 16), _clk_) AND PC' = 94;
36  PC = 94 -> PC' = 75;
37  PC = 95 -> PC' = 96;
38  PC = 96 -> 2_reg' = gp_reg +U getGlobalIndex(data1Ready) AND
```

```
39  |                  PC' = 97;
40  | PC = 97 -> lw(4_reg', memAdr(2_reg, 0), _clk_) AND PC' = 98;
41  | PC = 98 -> ra_reg' = 100 AND PC' = 11;
42  | PC = 99 -> PC' = 100;
43  | PC = 100 -> 2_reg' = 0 +U 3 AND PC' = 101;
44  | PC = 101 -> lw(3_reg', memAdr(sp_reg, 16), _clk_) AND PC' = 102;
45  | PC = 102 -> 2_reg' = 2_reg < 3_reg AND PC' = 103;
46  | PC = 103 AND 2_reg != 0 -> PC' = 121;
47  | PC = 104 -> PC' = 105;
48  | PC = 105 -> PC' = 107;
49  | PC = 106 -> PC' = 107;
50  | PC = 107 -> lw(4_reg', memAdr(sp_reg, 16), _clk_) AND PC' = 108;
51  | PC = 108 -> ra_reg' = 110 AND PC' = 22;
52  | PC = 109 -> PC' = 110;
53  | PC = 110 -> 4_reg' = gp_reg +U getGlobalIndex(sensors) AND
54  |                  PC' = 111;
55  | PC = 111 -> lw(3_reg', memAdr(sp_reg, 16), _clk_) AND PC' = 112;
56  | PC = 112 -> lw(4_reg', memAdr(4_reg, 0), _clk_) AND PC' = 113;
57  | PC = 113 -> 3_reg' = 3_reg << 2 AND PC' = 114;
58  | PC = 114 -> 3_reg' = 4_reg +U 3_reg AND PC' = 115;
59  | PC = 115 -> sw(2_reg, memAdr(3_reg, 0), _clk_) AND PC' = 116;
60  | PC = 116 -> lw(2_reg', memAdr(sp_reg, 16), _clk_) AND PC' = 117;
61  | PC = 117 -> 2_reg' = 2_reg +U 1 AND PC' = 118;
62  | PC = 118 -> sw(2_reg, memAdr(sp_reg, 16), _clk_) AND PC' = 119;
63  | PC = 119 -> PC' = 100;
64  | PC = 120 -> PC' = 121;
65  | PC = 121 -> 2_reg' = gp_reg +U getGlobalIndex(data2Ready) AND
66  |                  PC' = 122;
67  | PC = 122 -> lw(4_reg', memAdr(2_reg, 0), _clk_) AND PC' = 123;
68  | PC = 123 -> ra_reg' = 125 AND PC' = 11;
69  | PC = 124 -> PC' = 125;
70  | PC = 125 -> lw(ra_reg', memAdr(sp_reg, 20), _clk_) AND
71  |                  PC' = 126;
72  | PC = 126 -> sp_reg' = sp_reg +U 24 AND resetMem(sp_reg, 24) AND
73  |                  PC' = 127;
```

```
74  PC = 127 -> PC' = ra_reg;
75  PC = 128 -> PC' = 129;
```

Listing A.5. The MEMICS Model for the Function writeOutputs from Example 2.3.1 in Chapter 2

```
1   PC = 129 -> PC' = 130;
2   PC = 130 -> PC' = 131;
3   PC = 131 -> sp_reg' = sp_reg +U 4294967256 AND PC' = 132;
4   PC = 132 -> sw(ra_reg, memAdr(sp_reg, 36), _clk_) AND PC' = 133;
5   PC = 133 -> 2_reg' = gp_reg +U getGlobalIndex(worker1Ready) AND
6              PC' = 134;
7   PC = 134 -> lw(2_reg', memAdr(2_reg, 0), _clk_) AND PC' = 135;
8   PC = 135 -> lw(4_reg', memAdr(2_reg, 0), _clk_) AND PC' = 136;
9   PC = 136 -> 2_reg' = gp_reg +U getGlobalIndex(worker2Ready) AND
10             PC' = 137;
11  PC = 137 -> lw(2_reg', memAdr(2_reg, 0), _clk_) AND PC' = 138;
12  PC = 138 -> sw(2_reg, memAdr(sp_reg, 28), _clk_) AND PC' = 139;
13  PC = 139 AND waitOnEvent(worker1Ready)-> PC' = 140;
14  PC = 140 -> PC' = 141;
15  PC = 141 -> lw(4_reg', memAdr(sp_reg, 28), _clk_) AND PC' = 142;
16  PC = 142 -> lw(4_reg', memAdr(4_reg, 0), _clk_) AND PC' = 143;
17  PC = 143 -> sw(2_reg, memAdr(sp_reg, 24), _clk_) AND PC' = 144;
18  PC = 144 AND waitOnEvent(worker2Ready)-> PC' = 145;
19  PC = 145 -> PC' = 146;
20  PC = 146 -> sw(0, memAdr(sp_reg, 32), _clk_) AND PC' = 147;
21  PC = 147 -> sw(2_reg, memAdr(sp_reg, 20), _clk_) AND PC' = 148;
22  PC = 148 -> 2_reg' = 0 +U 3 AND PC' = 149;
23  PC = 149 -> lw(3_reg', memAdr(sp_reg, 32), _clk_) AND PC' = 150;
24  PC = 150 -> 2_reg' = 2_reg < 3_reg AND PC' = 151;
25  PC = 151 AND 2_reg != 0 -> PC' = 170;
26  PC = 152 -> PC' = 153;
27  PC = 153 -> PC' = 155;
28  PC = 154 -> PC' = 155;
29  PC = 155 -> 2_reg' = gp_reg +U getGlobalIndex(tmp) AND
```

```
30  │                   PC' = 156;
31  │ PC = 156 -> lw(3_reg', memAdr(sp_reg, 32), _clk_) AND PC' = 157;
32  │ PC = 157 -> 4_reg' = gp_reg +U getGlobalIndex(actors) AND
33  │                   PC' = 158;
34  │ PC = 158 -> lw(2_reg', memAdr(2_reg, 0), _clk_) AND PC' = 159;
35  │ PC = 159 -> 3_reg' = 3_reg << 2 AND PC' = 160;
36  │ PC = 160 -> 2_reg' = 2_reg +U 3_reg AND PC' = 161;
37  │ PC = 161 -> lw(4_reg', memAdr(4_reg, 0), _clk_) AND PC' = 162;
38  │ PC = 162 -> lw(2_reg', memAdr(2_reg, 0), _clk_) AND PC' = 163;
39  │ PC = 163 -> 3_reg' = 4_reg +U 3_reg AND PC' = 164;
40  │ PC = 164 -> sw(2_reg, memAdr(3_reg, 0), _clk_) AND PC' = 165;
41  │ PC = 165 -> lw(2_reg', memAdr(sp_reg, 32), _clk_) AND PC' = 166;
42  │ PC = 166 -> 2_reg' = 2_reg +U 1 AND PC' = 167;
43  │ PC = 167 -> sw(2_reg, memAdr(sp_reg, 32), _clk_) AND PC' = 168;
44  │ PC = 168 -> PC' = 148;
45  │ PC = 169 -> PC' = 170;
46  │ PC = 170 -> lw(ra_reg', memAdr(sp_reg, 36), _clk_) AND
47  │                   PC' = 171;
48  │ PC = 171 -> sp_reg' = sp_reg +U 40 AND resetMem(sp_reg, 40) AND
49  │                   PC' = 172;
50  │ PC = 172 -> PC' = ra_reg;
51  │ PC = 173 -> PC' = 174;
```

Listing A.6. The MEMICS Model for the Function worker1 from Example 2.3.1 in Chapter 2

```
1  │ PC = 174 -> PC' = 175;
2  │ PC = 175 -> PC' = 176;
3  │ PC = 176 -> sp_reg' = sp_reg +U 4294967240 AND PC' = 177;
4  │ PC = 177 -> sw(ra_reg, memAdr(sp_reg, 52), _clk_) AND PC' = 178;
5  │ PC = 178 -> 2_reg' = gp_reg +U getGlobalIndex(worker1Ready) AND
6  │                   PC' = 179;
7  │ PC = 179 -> 3_reg' = gp_reg +U getGlobalIndex(data1Ready) AND
8  │                   PC' = 180;
9  │ PC = 180 -> lw(4_reg', memAdr(2_reg, 0), _clk_) AND PC' = 181;
```

```
10  PC = 181 -> lw(2_reg', memAdr(3_reg, 0), _clk_) AND PC' = 182;
11  PC = 182 -> sw(2_reg, memAdr(sp_reg, 40), _clk_) AND PC' = 183;
12  PC = 183 -> ra_reg' = 185 AND PC' = 1;
13  PC = 184 -> PC' = 185;
14  PC = 185 -> lw(2_reg', memAdr(sp_reg, 40), _clk_) AND PC' = 186;
15  PC = 186 -> lw(4_reg', memAdr(2_reg, 0), _clk_) AND PC' = 187;
16  PC = 187 AND waitOnEvent(dataReady)-> PC' = 188;
17  PC = 188 -> PC' = 189;
18  PC = 189 -> 3_reg' = 0 +U 2 AND PC' = 190;
19  PC = 190 -> sw(0, memAdr(sp_reg, 48), _clk_) AND PC' = 191;
20  PC = 191 -> sw(3_reg, memAdr(sp_reg, 44), _clk_) AND PC' = 192;
21  PC = 192 -> sw(2_reg, memAdr(sp_reg, 36), _clk_) AND PC' = 193;
22  PC = 193 -> lw(2_reg', memAdr(sp_reg, 48), _clk_) AND PC' = 194;
23  PC = 194 -> lw(3_reg', memAdr(sp_reg, 44), _clk_) AND PC' = 195;
24  PC = 195 -> 2_reg' = 2_reg < 3_reg AND PC' = 196;
25  PC = 196 AND 2_reg == 0 -> PC' = 242;
26  PC = 197 -> PC' = 198;
27  PC = 198 -> PC' = 200;
28  PC = 199 -> PC' = 200;
29  PC = 200 -> lw(4_reg', memAdr(sp_reg, 48), _clk_) AND PC' = 201;
30  PC = 201 -> 2_reg' = 0 +U 4 AND PC' = 202;
31  PC = 202 -> 5_reg' = 0 +U 2_reg AND PC' = 203;
32  PC = 203 -> sw(2_reg, memAdr(sp_reg, 32), _clk_) AND PC' = 204;
33  PC = 204 -> ra_reg' = 206 AND PC' = 31;
34  PC = 205 -> PC' = 206;
35  PC = 206 -> 4_reg' = gp_reg +U getGlobalIndex(sensors) AND
36              PC' = 207;
37  PC = 207 -> lw(5_reg', memAdr(sp_reg, 48), _clk_) AND PC' = 208;
38  PC = 208 -> 2_reg' = 2_reg << 2 AND PC' = 209;
39  PC = 209 -> lw(4_reg', memAdr(4_reg, 0), _clk_) AND PC' = 210;
40  PC = 210 -> 3_reg' = 5_reg << 2 AND PC' = 211;
41  PC = 211 -> 2_reg' = 4_reg +U 2_reg AND PC' = 212;
42  PC = 212 -> 3_reg' = 4_reg +U 3_reg AND PC' = 213;
43  PC = 213 -> lw(3_reg', memAdr(3_reg, 0), _clk_) AND PC' = 214;
44  PC = 214 -> lw(2_reg', memAdr(2_reg, 0), _clk_) AND PC' = 215;
```

A. The MEMICS Model for the Automotive Example 2.3.1

```
45   PC = 215 -> sw(4_reg, memAdr(sp_reg, 28), _clk_) AND PC' = 216;
46   PC = 216 -> 4_reg' = 0 +U 5_reg AND PC' = 217;
47   PC = 217 -> lw(5_reg', memAdr(sp_reg, 32), _clk_) AND PC' = 218;
48   PC = 218 -> sw(2_reg, memAdr(sp_reg, 24), _clk_) AND PC' = 219;
49   PC = 219 -> sw(3_reg, memAdr(sp_reg, 20), _clk_) AND PC' = 220;
50   PC = 220 -> ra_reg' = 222 AND PC' = 47;
51   PC = 221 -> PC' = 222;
52   PC = 222 -> 2_reg' = 2_reg << 2 AND PC' = 223;
53   PC = 223 -> lw(3_reg', memAdr(sp_reg, 20), _clk_) AND PC' = 224;
54   PC = 224 -> 3_reg' = 3_reg << 1 AND PC' = 225;
55   PC = 225 -> 4_reg' = gp_reg +U getGlobalIndex(tmp) AND
56               PC' = 226;
57   PC = 226 -> lw(5_reg', memAdr(sp_reg, 28), _clk_) AND PC' = 227;
58   PC = 227 -> 2_reg' = 5_reg +U 2_reg AND PC' = 228;
59   PC = 228 -> lw(6_reg', memAdr(sp_reg, 48), _clk_) AND PC' = 229;
60   PC = 229 -> lw(2_reg', memAdr(2_reg, 0), _clk_) AND PC' = 230;
61   PC = 230 -> lw(7_reg', memAdr(sp_reg, 24), _clk_) AND PC' = 231;
62   PC = 231 -> 3_reg' = 7_reg -U 3_reg AND PC' = 232;
63   PC = 232 -> lw(4_reg', memAdr(4_reg, 0), _clk_) AND PC' = 233;
64   PC = 233 -> 6_reg' = 6_reg << 2 AND PC' = 234;
65   PC = 234 -> 2_reg' = 3_reg +U 2_reg AND PC' = 235;
66   PC = 235 -> 3_reg' = 4_reg +U 6_reg AND PC' = 236;
67   PC = 236 -> sw(2_reg, memAdr(3_reg, 0), _clk_) AND PC' = 237;
68   PC = 237 -> lw(2_reg', memAdr(sp_reg, 48), _clk_) AND PC' = 238;
69   PC = 238 -> 2_reg' = 2_reg +U 1 AND PC' = 239;
70   PC = 239 -> sw(2_reg, memAdr(sp_reg, 48), _clk_) AND PC' = 240;
71   PC = 240 -> PC' = 193;
72   PC = 241 -> PC' = 242;
73   PC = 242 -> 2_reg' = gp_reg +U getGlobalIndex(worker1Ready) AND
74               PC' = 243;
75   PC = 243 -> lw(4_reg', memAdr(2_reg, 0), _clk_) AND PC' = 244;
76   PC = 244 -> ra_reg' = 246 AND PC' = 11;
77   PC = 245 -> PC' = 246;
78   PC = 246 -> lw(ra_reg', memAdr(sp_reg, 52), _clk_) AND
79               PC' = 247;
```

```
80   PC = 247 -> sp_reg' = sp_reg +U 56 AND resetMem(sp_reg, 56) AND
81               PC' = 248;
82   PC = 248 -> PC' = ra_reg;
83   PC = 249 -> PC' = 250;
```

Listing A.7. The MEMICS Model for the Function worker2 from Example 2.3.1 in Chapter 2

```
 1   PC = 250 -> PC' = 251;
 2   PC = 251 -> PC' = 252;
 3   PC = 252 -> sp_reg' = sp_reg +U 4294967240 AND PC' = 253;
 4   PC = 253 -> sw(ra_reg, memAdr(sp_reg, 52), _clk_) AND PC' = 254;
 5   PC = 254 -> 2_reg' = gp_reg +U getGlobalIndex(worker2Ready) AND
 6               PC' = 255;
 7   PC = 255 -> 3_reg' = gp_reg +U getGlobalIndex(data2Ready) AND
 8               PC' = 256;
 9   PC = 256 -> lw(4_reg', memAdr(2_reg, 0), _clk_) AND PC' = 257;
10   PC = 257 -> lw(2_reg', memAdr(3_reg, 0), _clk_) AND PC' = 258;
11   PC = 258 -> sw(2_reg, memAdr(sp_reg, 44), _clk_) AND PC' = 259;
12   PC = 259 -> ra_reg' = 261 AND PC' = 1;
13   PC = 260 -> PC' = 261;
14   PC = 261 -> lw(2_reg', memAdr(sp_reg, 44), _clk_) AND PC' = 262;
15   PC = 262 -> lw(4_reg', memAdr(2_reg, 0), _clk_) AND PC' = 263;
16   PC = 263 -> 2_reg' = 0 +U 2 AND PC' = 264;
17   PC = 264 -> sw(2_reg, memAdr(sp_reg, 40), _clk_) AND PC' = 265;
18   PC = 265 AND waitOnEvent(data2Ready)-> PC' = 266;
19   PC = 266 -> PC' = 267;
20   PC = 267 -> lw(3_reg', memAdr(sp_reg, 40), _clk_) AND PC' = 268;
21   PC = 268 -> sw(3_reg, memAdr(sp_reg, 48), _clk_) AND PC' = 269;
22   PC = 269 -> sw(2_reg, memAdr(sp_reg, 36), _clk_) AND PC' = 270;
23   PC = 270 -> 2_reg' = 0 +U 3 AND PC' = 271;
24   PC = 271 -> lw(3_reg', memAdr(sp_reg, 48), _clk_) AND PC' = 272;
25   PC = 272 -> 2_reg' = 2_reg < 3_reg AND PC' = 273;
26   PC = 273 AND 2_reg != 0 -> PC' = 319;
27   PC = 274 -> PC' = 275;
```

A. The MEMICS Model for the Automotive Example 2.3.1

```
28  PC = 275 -> PC' = 277;
29  PC = 276 -> PC' = 277;
30  PC = 277 -> lw(4_reg', memAdr(sp_reg, 48), _clk_) AND PC' = 278;
31  PC = 278 -> 2_reg' = 0 +U 4 AND PC' = 279;
32  PC = 279 -> 5_reg' = 0 +U 2_reg AND PC' = 280;
33  PC = 280 -> sw(2_reg, memAdr(sp_reg, 32), _clk_) AND PC' = 281;
34  PC = 281 -> ra_reg' = 283 AND PC' = 31;
35  PC = 282 -> PC' = 283;
36  PC = 283 -> 4_reg' = gp_reg +U getGlobalIndex(sensors) AND
37               PC' = 284;
38  PC = 284 -> lw(5_reg', memAdr(sp_reg, 48), _clk_) AND PC' = 285;
39  PC = 285 -> 2_reg' = 2_reg << 2 AND PC' = 286;
40  PC = 286 -> lw(4_reg', memAdr(4_reg, 0), _clk_) AND PC' = 287;
41  PC = 287 -> 3_reg' = 5_reg << 2 AND PC' = 288;
42  PC = 288 -> 2_reg' = 4_reg +U 2_reg AND PC' = 289;
43  PC = 289 -> 3_reg' = 4_reg +U 3_reg AND PC' = 290;
44  PC = 290 -> lw(3_reg', memAdr(3_reg, 0), _clk_) AND PC' = 291;
45  PC = 291 -> lw(2_reg', memAdr(2_reg, 0), _clk_) AND PC' = 292;
46  PC = 292 -> sw(4_reg, memAdr(sp_reg, 28), _clk_) AND PC' = 293;
47  PC = 293 -> 4_reg' = 0 +U 5_reg AND PC' = 294;
48  PC = 294 -> lw(5_reg', memAdr(sp_reg, 32), _clk_) AND PC' = 295;
49  PC = 295 -> sw(2_reg, memAdr(sp_reg, 24), _clk_) AND PC' = 296;
50  PC = 296 -> sw(3_reg, memAdr(sp_reg, 20), _clk_) AND PC' = 297;
51  PC = 297 -> ra_reg' = 299 AND PC' = 47;
52  PC = 298 -> PC' = 299;
53  PC = 299 -> 2_reg' = 2_reg << 2 AND PC' = 300;
54  PC = 300 -> lw(3_reg', memAdr(sp_reg, 20), _clk_) AND PC' = 301;
55  PC = 301 -> 3_reg' = 3_reg << 1 AND PC' = 302;
56  PC = 302 -> 4_reg' = gp_reg +U getGlobalIndex(tmp) AND
57               PC' = 303;
58  PC = 303 -> lw(5_reg', memAdr(sp_reg, 28), _clk_) AND PC' = 304;
59  PC = 304 -> 2_reg' = 5_reg +U 2_reg AND PC' = 305;
60  PC = 305 -> lw(6_reg', memAdr(sp_reg, 48), _clk_) AND PC' = 306;
61  PC = 306 -> lw(2_reg', memAdr(2_reg, 0), _clk_) AND PC' = 307;
62  PC = 307 -> lw(7_reg', memAdr(sp_reg, 24), _clk_) AND PC' = 308;
```

```
63  PC = 308 -> 3_reg' = 7_reg -U 3_reg AND PC' = 309;
64  PC = 309 -> lw(4_reg', memAdr(4_reg, 0), _clk_) AND PC' = 310;
65  PC = 310 -> 6_reg' = 6_reg << 2 AND PC' = 311;
66  PC = 311 -> 2_reg' = 3_reg +U 2_reg AND PC' = 312;
67  PC = 312 -> 3_reg' = 4_reg +U 6_reg AND PC' = 313;
68  PC = 313 -> sw(2_reg, memAdr(3_reg, 0), _clk_) AND PC' = 314;
69  PC = 314 -> lw(2_reg', memAdr(sp_reg, 48), _clk_) AND PC' = 315;
70  PC = 315 -> 2_reg' = 2_reg +U 1 AND PC' = 316;
71  PC = 316 -> sw(2_reg, memAdr(sp_reg, 48), _clk_) AND PC' = 317;
72  PC = 317 -> PC' = 270;
73  PC = 318 -> PC' = 319;
74  PC = 319 -> 2_reg' = gp_reg +U getGlobalIndex(worker2Ready) AND
75             PC' = 320;
76  PC = 320 -> lw(4_reg', memAdr(2_reg, 0), _clk_) AND PC' = 321;
77  PC = 321 -> ra_reg' = 323 AND PC' = 11;
78  PC = 322 -> PC' = 323;
79  PC = 323 -> lw(ra_reg', memAdr(sp_reg, 52), _clk_) AND
80             PC' = 324;
81  PC = 324 -> sp_reg' = sp_reg +U 56 AND resetMem(sp_reg, 56) AND
82             PC' = 325;
83  PC = 325 -> PC' = ra_reg;
84  PC = 326 -> PC' = 327;
```

The MEMICS Instruction Set

Table B.1. MEMICS Instruction Set: Floating Point Instructions
All Instructions in this Table are operating on Floating Point Registers.

Instruction	Description
$a'_{fp} := fadd(b_{fp}, c_{fp})$;	The values of the registers b_{fp} and c_{fp} are added and stored into the register a_{fp}.
$a'_{fp} := fsub(b_{fp}, c_{fp})$;	The values of the registers b_{fp} and c_{fp} are subtracted and stored into the register a_{fp}.
$a'_{fp} := fmul(b_{fp}, c_{fp})$;	The values of the registers b_{fp} and c_{fp} are multiplied and stored into the register a_{fp}.
$a'_{fp} := fdiv(b_{fp}, c_{fp})$;	The value of the register b_{fp} is divided by the value of the register c_{fp} and the result is stored into the register a_{fp}.
$a'_{fp} := fexp(b_{fp})$;	The exponential function for the value of register b_{fp} is computed and stored into the register a_{fp}.
$a'_{fp} := fpow(b_{fp}, c_{fp})$;	The power function of the value from register b_{fp} to the basis of the value in register c_{fp} is computed and stored into the register a_{fp}.
$a'_{fp} := flog(b_{fp})$;	The logarithm of the value from register b_{fp} is computed and store in register a_{fp}.
$a'_{fp} := fsqrt(b_{fp})$;	The square-root of the value in register b_{fp} is computed and stored in register a_{fp}.
$a'_{fp} := fnroot(b_{fp}, c_{fp})$;	The nth-root of the value in register b_{fp}, where n is defined by the value in register c, is assigned to the register a_{fp}.

B. The MEMICS Instruction Set

$a'_{fp} := \text{fabs}(b_{fp});$	The absolute value of the value in register b_{fp} is assigned to the register a_{fp}.
$a'_{fp} := \text{fmin}(b_{fp}, c_{fp});$	The minimum of the two values from register b_{fp} and c_{fp} is assigned to the register a_{fp}.
$a'_{fp} := \text{fmax}(b_{fp}, c_{fp});$	The maximum of the two values from register b_{fp} and c_{fp} is assigned to the register a_{fp}.
$a'_{fp} := \text{fcos}(b_{fp});$	The cosine value of the value from register b_{fp} is stored into register a_{fp}.
$a'_{fp} := \text{ftan}(b_{fp});$	The sine value of the value from register b_{fp} is stored into register a_{fp}.
$a'_{fp} := \text{fsin}(b_{fp});$	The tangent value of the value from register b_{fp} is stored into register a_{fp}.
$a'_{fp} := \text{farccos}(b_{fp});$	The arc cosine value of the value from register b_{fp} is stored into register a_{fp}.
$a'_{fp} := \text{farctan}(b_{fp});$	The arc sine value of the value from register b_{fp} is stored into register a_{fp}.
$a'_{fp} := \text{farcsin}(b_{fp});$	The arc tangent value of the value from register b_{fp} is stored into register a_{fp}.

Table B.2. MEMICS Instruction Set: Unsigned Integer Instructions – Arithmetic

Instruction	Description
$a' := \text{addu}(b, c);$	The values of the registers b and c are added and stored into the register a.
$a' := \text{subu}(b, c);$	The values of the registers b and c are subtracted and stored into the register a.
$a' := \text{mulu}(b, c);$	The values of the registers b and c are multiplied and stored into the register a.
$a' := \text{divu}(b, c);$	The value of the registers b is divided by the value of the register c and the result is stored into the register a.
$a' := \text{expu}(b);$	The exponential function for the value of register b is computed and stored into the register a.

a′ := powu(b, c);	The power function of the value from register b to the basis of the value in register c is computed and stored into the register a.
a′ := logu(b);	The logarithm of the value from register b is computed and store in register a.
a′ := sqrtu(b);	The square-root of the value in register b is computed and stored in register a.
a′ := nrootu(b, c);	The nth-root of the value in register b, where n is defined by the value in register c, is assigned to the register a.
a′ := absu(b);	The absolute value of the value in register b is assigned to the register a.
a′ := minu(b, c);	The minimum of the two values from register b and c is assigned to the register a.
a′ := maxu(b, c);	The maximum of the two values from register b and c is assigned to the register a.
a′ := cosu(b);	The cosine value of the value from register b is stored into register a.
a′ := tanu(b);	The sine value of the value from register b is stored into register a.
a′ := sinu(b);	The tangent value of the value from register b is stored into register a.
a′ := arccosu(b);	The arc cosine value of the value from register b is stored into register a.
a′ := arctanu(b);	The arc sine value of the value from register b is stored into register a.
a′ := arcsinu(b);	The arc tangent value of the value from register b is stored into register a.

Bibliography

[1] B. W. Kernighan, *The C Programming Language*, 2nd ed., D. M. Ritchie, Ed. Prentice Hall Professional Technical Reference, 1988.

[2] B. Stroustrup, *The C++ Programming Language, 4th Edition*, 4th ed. Addison-Wesley Professional, May 2013.

[3] J. Martin, *Programming real-time computer systems*, ser. Prentice-Hall series in automatic computation. Prentice-Hall, 1965.

[4] A. Burns and A. J. Wellings, *Real-Time Systems and Programming Languages: ADA 95, Real-Time Java, and Real-Time POSIX*, 3rd ed. Boston, MA, USA: Addison-Wesley Longman Publishing Co., Inc., 2001.

[5] *OSEK*, http://portal.osek-vdx.org.

[6] OSEK group, *OSEK/VDX - Operating System*, http://portal.osek-vdx.org/files/pdf/specs/oil25.pdf, 2005.

[7] ——, *OSEK/VDX - System Generation - OIL: OSEK Implementation Language*, http://portal.osek-vdx.org/files/pdf/specs/oil25.pdf, 2004.

[8] L. Sha, J. P. Lehoczky, and R. Rajkumar, "Priority inheritance protocols an approach to real-time synchronization," Carnegie-Mellon University.Computer science. Pittsburgh (PA US), Tech. Rep. CMU-CS-87-181, 1987. [Online]. Available: http://opac.inria.fr/record=b1021218

[9] L. Sha, R. Rajkumar, and J. Lehoczky, "Priority inheritance protocols: an approach to real-time synchronization," *Computers, IEEE Transactions on*, vol. 39, no. 9, pp. 1175–1185, Sep 1990.

[10] Autosar Consortium, *AUTOSAR - Specification of Operating System*, http://autosar.org.

Bibliography

[11] "ISO/DIS 26262-1 - Road vehicles — Functional safety — Part 1 Glossary," Geneva, Switzerland, Tech. Rep., Jul. 2009.

[12] S. Höppner and A. Rausch, "V-Modell XT - eine Einführung," *Schriften zum Software-Qualitätsmanagement, Vorgehen, Methoden und Werkzeuge für die Software-Qualitätssicherung*, 2005.

[13] R. Höhn and S. Höppner, Eds., *Das V-Modell XT: Grundlagen, Methodik und Anwendungen*. Berlin: Springer, 2008.

[14] *Common Weakness Enumeration*, http://cwe.mitre.org.

[15] R. C. Gonzalez and R. E. Woods, *Digital Image Processing*, 2nd ed. Boston, MA, USA: Addison-Wesley Longman Publishing Co., Inc., 2001.

[16] A. M. Turing, "On Computable Numbers, with an Application to the Entscheidungsproblem," *Proceedings of the London Mathematical Society*, vol. 2, no. 42, pp. 230–265, 1936.

[17] J. E. Hopcroft, R. Motwani, and J. D. Ullman, *Introduction to Automata Theory, Languages, and Computation (3rd Edition)*. Boston, MA, USA: Addison-Wesley Longman Publishing Co., Inc., 2006.

[18] P. Cousot and R. Cousot, "Abstract interpretation: a unified lattice model for static analysis of programs by construction or approximation of fixpoints," in *Proceedings of the 4th ACM SIGACT-SIGPLAN symposium on Principles of programming languages*, ser. POPL '77. New York, NY, USA: ACM, 1977, pp. 238–252.

[19] M. Sintzoff, "Calculating properties of programs by valuations on specific models," in *Proceedings of ACM conference on Proving assertions about programs*. New York, NY, USA: ACM, 1972, pp. 203–207.

[20] U. Khedker, A. Sanyal, and B. Karkare, *Data Flow Analysis: Theory and Practice*, 1st ed. Boca Raton, FL, USA: CRC Press, Inc., 2009.

[21] G. A. Kildall, "Global expression optimization during compilation," Ph.D. dissertation, 1972.

[22] J. Kam and J. Ullman, "Monotone data flow analysis frameworks," *Acta Informatica*, vol. 7, no. 3, pp. 305–317, 1977.

[23] M. N. Wegman and F. K. Zadeck, "Constant propagation with conditional branches," in *Proceedings of the 12th ACM SIGACT-SIGPLAN symposium on Principles of programming languages*, ser. POPL '85. New York, NY, USA: ACM, 1985, pp. 291–299.

[24] E. M. Clarke, Jr., O. Grumberg, and D. A. Peled, *Model checking*. Cambridge, MA, USA: MIT Press, 1999.

[25] C. Baier and J.-P. Katoen, *Principles of Model Checking*. The MIT Press, 2008.

[26] A. Biere, A. Cimatti, E. M. Clarke, O. Strichman, and Y. Zhu, "Bounded model checking," ser. Advances in Computers. Elsevier, 2003, vol. 58, pp. 117 – 148.

[27] M. Fitting, *First-Order Logic and Automated Theorem Proving*, ser. Graduate texts in computer science. Springer, 1996.

[28] S. A. Cook, "The complexity of theorem-proving procedures," in *Proceedings of the third annual ACM symposium on Theory of computing*, ser. STOC '71. New York, NY, USA: ACM, 1971, pp. 151–158.

[29] D. Kroening and O. Strichman, *Decision Procedures: An Algorithmic Point of View*, 1st ed. Springer Publishing Company, Incorporated, 2008.

[30] M. Davis and H. Putnam, "A Computing Procedure for Quantification Theory," *J. ACM*, vol. 7, no. 3, pp. 201–215, Jul. 1960.

[31] M. Davis, G. Logemann, and D. Loveland, "A machine program for theorem-proving," *Commun. ACM*, vol. 5, pp. 394–397, July 1962.

[32] M. W. Moskewicz, C. F. Madigan, Y. Zhao, L. Zhang, and S. Malik, "Chaff: engineering an efficient SAT solver," in *Proceedings of the 38th annual Design Automation Conference*, ser. DAC '01. New York, NY, USA: ACM, 2001, pp. 530–535.

[33] L. de Moura and N. Bjørner, "Satisfiability Modulo Theories: An Appetizer," in *Formal Methods: Foundations and Applications*, M. V. Oliveira and J. Woodcock, Eds. Berlin, Heidelberg: Springer Berlin Heidelberg, 2009, vol. 5902, ch. 3, pp. 23–36.

[34] C. Barrett, A. Stump, C. Tinelli, S. Boehme, D. Cok, D. Deharbe, B. Dutertre, P. Fontaine, V. Ganesh, A. Griggio, J. Grundy, P. Jackson, A. Oliveras, S. Krstić, M. Moskal, L. D. Moura, R. Sebastiani, T. D. Cok, and J. Hoenicke, "C.: The SMT-LIB Standard: Version 2.0," Tech. Rep., 2010.

[35] L. Cordeiro, J. Morse, D. Nicole, and B. Fischer, "Context-Bounded model checking with ESBMC 1.17," in *Proceedings of the 18th international conference on Tools and Algorithms for the Construction and Analysis of Systems*, ser. TACAS'12. Berlin, Heidelberg: Springer-Verlag, 2012, pp. 534–537.

[36] C. Sinz, S. Falke, and F. Merz, "A Precise Memory Model for Low-Level Bounded Model Checking," in *Proceedings of the 5th International Workshop on Systems Software Verification (SSV '10)*, Vancouver, Canada, 2010.

[37] E. Hyvönen, "Constraint Reasoning Based on Interval Arithmetic: The Tolerance Propagation Approach," *Artif. Intell.*, vol. 58, no. 1-3, pp. 71–112, Dec. 1992.

[38] U. Montanari, "Networks of constraints: Fundamental properties and applications to picture processing," *Information Sciences*, vol. 7, no. 0, pp. 95 – 132, 1974.

[39] D. Waltz, "Understanding Line Drawings of Scenes with Shadows," in *The Psychology of Computer Vision*, P. H. Winston, Ed. McGraw-Hill, 1975, p. pages.

[40] A. K. Mackworth, "Consistency in networks of relations," *Artificial Intelligence*, vol. 8, no. 1, pp. 99 – 118, 1977.

[41] M. Fränzle, C. Herde, T. Teige, S. Ratschan, and T. Schubert, "Efficient solving of large non-linear arithmetic constraint systems with complex boolean structure," *Journal on Satisfiability, Boolean Modeling and Computation*, vol. 1, pp. 209–236, 2007.

[42] J. Traub, "Program Analysis and Probabilistic SAT-Solving," Master's thesis, Universität Stuttgart, 2010.

[43] R. Brooker, I. MacCallum, D. Morris, and J. Rohl, "The compiler compiler." *Annual Review in Automatic Programming*, pp. 3:229–275, 1963.

[44] A. V. Aho and J. D. Ullman, *Principles of Compiler Design (Addison-Wesley series in computer science and information processing)*. Boston, MA, USA: Addison-Wesley Longman Publishing Co., Inc., 1977.

[45] C. Lattner and V. Adve, "LLVM: A Compilation Framework for Lifelong Program Analysis & Transformation," in *Proceedings of the 2004 International Symposium on Code Generation and Optimization (CGO'04)*, Palo Alto, California, Mar 2004.

[46] D. Fandrey, "Clang/LLVM Maturity Report," June 2010, *See* http://www.iwi.hs-karlsruhe.de.

[47] C. Lattner, *LLVM Language Reference Manual*, http://llvm.org/docs/LangRef.html.

[48] D. Sweetman, *See MIPS Run, Second Edition*. San Francisco, CA, USA: Morgan Kaufmann Publishers Inc., 2006.

[49] B. Alpern, M. N. Wegman, and F. K. Zadeck, "Detecting equality of variables in programs," in *Proceedings of the 15th ACM SIGPLAN-SIGACT Symposium on Principles of Programming Languages*, 1988, pp. 1–11.

[50] B. K. Rosen, M. N. Wegman, and F. K. Zadeck, "Global value numbers and redundant computations," in *Proceedings of the 15th ACM SIGPLAN-SIGACT Symposium on Principles of Programming Languages*, 1988, pp. 12–27.

[51] D. A. Patterson and C. H. Séquin, "RISC I: A Reduced Instruction Set VLSI Computer." in *ISCA*, R. Y. Kain and W. R. Franta, Eds. IEEE Computer Society, 1981, pp. 443–458.

[52] J. Silc, B. Robič, and T. Ungerer, "CISC Processors," in *Processor Architecture*. Springer Berlin Heidelberg, 1999, pp. 99–122.

[53] D. Beyer, T. A. Henzinger, R. Jhala, and R. Majumdar, "The software model checker Blast: Applications to software engineering," *Int. J. Softw. Tools Technol. Transf.*, vol. 9, no. 5, pp. 505–525, Oct. 2007.

[54] E. Clarke, O. Grumberg, S. Jha, Y. Lu, and H. Veith, "Counterexample-Guided Abstraction Refinement," in *Computer Aided Verification*, ser. Lecture Notes in Computer Science, E. Emerson and A. Sistla, Eds. Springer Berlin Heidelberg, 2000, vol. 1855, pp. 154–169.

[55] T. A. Henzinger, R. Jhala, R. Majumdar, and G. Sutre, "Lazy abstraction," in *Proceedings of the 29th ACM SIGPLAN-SIGACT symposium on Principles of programming languages*, ser. POPL '02. New York, NY, USA: ACM, 2002, pp. 58–70.

[56] T. A. Henzinger, R. Jhala, R. Majumdar, and K. L. McMillan, "Abstractions from proofs," in *Proceedings of the 31st ACM SIGPLAN-SIGACT symposium on Principles of programming languages*, ser. POPL '04. New York, NY, USA: ACM, 2004, pp. 232–244.

[57] E. Clarke, D. Kroening, and F. Lerda, " A Tool for Checking ANSI-C Programs ," in *Tools and Algorithms for the Construction and Analysis of Systems (TACAS 2004)*, ser. Lecture Notes in Computer Science, K. Jensen and A. Podelski, Eds., vol. 2988. Springer, 2004, pp. 168–176.

[58] N. Eén and N. Sörensson, "An Extensible SAT-solver," in *SAT*, ser. Lecture Notes in Computer Science, E. Giunchiglia and A. Tacchella, Eds., vol. 2919. Springer, 2003, pp. 502–518.

[59] R. Brummayer and A. Biere, "Boolector: An Efficient SMT Solver for Bit-Vectors and Arrays," in *Proceedings of the 15th International Conference on Tools and Algorithms for the Construction and Analysis of Systems: Held as Part of the Joint European Conferences on Theory and Practice of Software, ETAPS 2009,*, ser. TACAS '09. Berlin, Heidelberg: Springer-Verlag, 2009, pp. 174–177.

[60] A. Cimatti, A. Griggio, B. Schaafsma, and R. Sebastiani, "The MathSAT5 SMT Solver," in *Tools and Algorithms for the Construction and Analysis of Systems*,

ser. Lecture Notes in Computer Science, N. Piterman and S. Smolka, Eds. Springer Berlin Heidelberg, 2013, vol. 7795, pp. 93–107.

[61] L. M. de Moura and N. Bjørner, "Z3: An Efficient SMT Solver," in *TACAS*, 2008, pp. 337–340.

[62] E. Clarke, D. Kroening, N. Sharygina, and K. Yorav, "SATABS: SAT-Based Predicate Abstraction for ANSI-C," in *Proceedings of the 11th International Conference on Tools and Algorithms for the Construction and Analysis of Systems*, ser. TACAS'05. Berlin, Heidelberg: Springer-Verlag, 2005, pp. 570–574.

[63] ——, " Predicate Abstraction of ANSI–C Programs using SAT ," *Formal Methods in System Design (FMSD)*, vol. 25, pp. 105–127, September–November 2004.

[64] S. Schwoon, "Model-Checking Pushdown Systems," Ph.D. dissertation, 2002.

[65] G. Holzmann, *Spin model checker, the: primer and reference manual*, 1st ed. Addison-Wesley Professional, 2003.

[66] A. Cimatti, E. Clarke, E. Giunchiglia, F. Giunchiglia, M. Pistore, M. Roveri, R. Sebastiani, and A. Tacchella, "NuSMV 2: An OpenSource Tool for Symbolic Model Checking," in *Computer Aided Verification*, ser. Lecture Notes in Computer Science, E. Brinksma and K. Larsen, Eds. Springer Berlin Heidelberg, 2002, vol. 2404, pp. 359–364.

[67] E. Clarke, D. Kroening, N. Sharygina, and K. Yorav, "Predicate Abstraction of ANSI-C Programs Using SAT," *Formal Methods in System Design*, vol. 25, no. 2-3, pp. 105–127, 2004.

[68] H. Jain, E. M. Clarke, and D. Kroening, "Verification of SpecC and Verilog using predicate abstraction," ser. MEMOCODE 2004. IEEE, 2004, pp. 7–16.

[69] E. Clarke, H. Jain, and D. Kroening, "Predicate abstraction and refinement techniques for verifying Verilog," Tech. Rep., 2004.

[70] V. Ganesh and D. L. Dill, "A decision procedure for bit-vectors and arrays," in *Proceedings of the 19th international conference on Computer aided verification*, ser. CAV'07. Berlin, Heidelberg: Springer-Verlag, 2007, pp. 519–531.

[71] K. Dudka, P. Müller, P. Peringer, and T. Vojnar, "Predator: A Verification Tool for Programs with Dynamic Linked Data Structures," in *Tools and Algorithms for the Construction and Analysis of Systems*, ser. Lecture Notes in Computer Science, C. Flanagan and B. König, Eds. Springer Berlin Heidelberg, 2012, vol. 7214, pp. 545–548.

[72] ——, "Predator: A Tool for Verification of Low-Level List Manipulation (Competition Contribution)," in *Tools and Algorithms for the Construction and Analysis of Systems*, ser. Lecture Notes in Computer Science Volume 7795, vol. 2013, no. 7795. Springer Verlag, 2013, pp. 627–629.

[73] A. Gupta, C. Popeea, and A. Rybalchenko, "Threader: A Constraint-Based Verifier for Multi-threaded Programs," in *CAV*, July 2011, pp. 412–417.

[74] G. Necula, S. McPeak, S. Rahul, and W. Weimer, "CIL: Intermediate Language and Tools for Analysis and Transformation of C Programs," in *Compiler Construction*, ser. Lecture Notes in Computer Science, R. Horspool, Ed. Springer Berlin Heidelberg, 2002, vol. 2304, pp. 213–228.

[75] B. Blanchet, P. Cousot, R. Cousot, J. Feret, L. Mauborgne, A. Miné, D. Monniaux, and X. Rival, "A Static Analyzer for Large Safety-critical Software," in *Proceedings of the ACM SIGPLAN 2003 Conference on Programming Language Design and Implementation*, ser. PLDI '03. New York, NY, USA: ACM, 2003, pp. 196–207.

[76] P. Cousot, R. Cousot, J. Feret, L. Mauborgne, A. Miné, D. Monniaux, and X. Rival, "The ASTRÉE analyzer," in *Programming Languages and Systems, Proceedings of the 14th European Symposium on Programming, volume 3444 of Lecture Notes in Computer Science*. Springer, 2005, pp. 21–30.

[77] D. Delmas and J. Souyris, "Astrée: From Research to Industry," in *Static Analysis*, ser. Lecture Notes in Computer Science, H. Nielson and G. Filé, Eds. Berlin, Heidelberg: Springer Berlin / Heidelberg, 2007, vol. 4634, ch. 27, pp. 437–451.

[78] P. Cousot, R. Cousot, J. Feret, L. Mauborgne, A. Miné, D. Monniaux, and X. Rival, "Combination of Abstractions in the ASTRÉE Static Analyzer." in *ASIAN*, ser. Lecture Notes in Computer Science, M. Okada and I. Satoh, Eds., vol. 4435. Springer, 2006, pp. 272–300.

[79] P. Cousot and R. Cousot, "Abstract interpretation frameworks," *Journal of Logic and Computation*, vol. 2, pp. 511–547, 1992.

[80] A. Raza, G. Vogel, and E. Plödereder, "Bauhaus - A Tool Suite for Program Analysis and Reverse Engineering," in *Reliable Software Technologies - Ada-Europe 2006*, ser. Lecture Notes in Computer Science, vol. 4006. Springer Berlin Heidelberg, 2006, pp. 71–82.

[81] MIRA Ltd, *MISRA-C:2004 Guidelines for the use of the C language in Critical Systems*, MIRA Std., Oct. 2004.

[82] S. Keul, "Tuning Static Data Race Analysis for Automotive Control Software," in *Source Code Analysis and Manipulation (SCAM), 2011 11th IEEE International Working Conference on*, 2011, pp. 45–54.

[83] *Polyspace*, http://www.mathworks.com/products/polyspace.

[84] D. Nowotka and J. Traub, "MEMICS - Memory Interval Constrain Solving of (concurrent) Machine Code," in *Automotive - Safety & Security 2012: Sicherheit und Zuverlässigkeit für automobile Informationstechnik*, ser. Lecture Notes in Informatics, E. Plödereder, P. Dencker, H. Klenk, H. B. Keller, and S. Spitzer, Eds., vol. 210. Springer, 2012, pp. 69 – 83.

[85] ——, "Formal Verification of Concurrent Embedded Software," in *Embedded Systems: Design, Analysis and Verification*, ser. IFIP Advances in Information and Communication Technology, G. Schirner, M. Götz, A. Rettberg, M. Zanella, and F. Rammig, Eds. Springer Berlin Heidelberg, 2013, vol. 403, pp. 218–227.

[86] T. Ehlers, D. Nowotka, P. Sieweck, and J. Traub, "Formal software verification for the migration of embedded code from single- to multicore systems," in *Software Engineering 2014: Fachtagung des GI-Fachbereichs Softwaretechnik*, ser. Lecture Notes in Informatics, W. Hasselbring and N. C. E. (Hrsg.), Eds., vol. 227, 2014, pp. 137 – 142.

[87] M. J. Eager and E. Consulting, "Introduction to the DWARF Debugging Format," *Group*, 2007.

[88] The DWARF committee, "DWARF Version 4 Released." 2010.

[89] *Competition on Software Verification (SV-Comp) 2013*, http://sv-comp.sosy-lab.org/2013/.

[90] Canonical Ltd., www.ubuntu.com.

[91] B. Nichols, D. Buttlar, and J. P. Farrell, *Pthreads programming*. Sebastopol, CA, USA: O'Reilly & Associates, Inc., 1996.